FISHING THE PEMBROKESHIRE COAST

*A guide to fishing the Pembrokeshire
coast from Machynys to St. Govens Head.*

By
Malcolm Halfpenny

2004

ISBN 0 9547079 0 7

Printed by Dinefwr Press
Rawlings Road, Llandybie
Carmarthenshire
SA18 3YD

With very special thanks to
my wife Patricia Anne for her perseverance.

This book is also dedicated to my very special family
Stephen, Michael, Estelle, Rhian, my grandchildren
Leigh and Rachel.

A very special thank you to
O. Mustad & Son. A.S.
Birgit N. Kallokkebakken
and 'Magne' of Mustad Hooks Norway,
for designing the book cover.

Contents

Beaches

Introduction

I like looking and reading maps, and have used THREE in the production of this book.

> LANDRANGER 158 – Tenby and Pembroke
> PATHFINDER 1105 – Pendine.
> PATHFINDER 1126 – Gower.

The maps are divided into a number of squares with the National Grid Numbers alongside (NGR).

To use the national grid numbers, read the numbers along the bottom first, and then the numbers upwards, where the lines intersect, read the national grid reference number. I have entered these in the book as **NGR.**

e.g.: to find **St. Govens Head (NGR 97.5/92.7)**

A guide to distance: map scale 1:50,000 – 1 mile equals one and a quarter inches, therefore, whilst doing your measurements one sixteenth of an inch equals 110 yards.

(NB: It is also important to buy the relevant tide table of the area being fished.)

Foreword

The Pembrokeshire Coastal path is approximately 168 miles long from POPPIT sands in the North to the NEW INN at AMROTH in the South, which divides the counties of Carmarthenshire and Pembrokeshire, but this fishing book takes you from MACHYNYS near LLANELLI to ST. GOVENS HEAD.

Remember the book is only a guide so always err on the side of safety. Rock fishing watch for the wave that takes you by surprise. Marshlands that will catch out the unwary, only fish these on neap tides. Seek out local knowledge, do not take chances!

Along the side of the road throughout Pembrokeshire were stones originally called "FINGER POSTS" for direction and distance, dating from 1694, sadly mostly gone, just the odd milestone left.

Machynys

Camping/Caravans	No
Disabled	No
Bait	Blow Lugworm, Crab, Mussel, Cockle
Seafood	Mussel, Cockle

Directions

From the Severn bridge area come off the M4 motorway at junction 47, take the A483 towards Swansea. At the next roundabout turn right onto the A484 towards LLANELLI. Follow the A484 across the Burry Estuary road bridge. Carry straight on at the next roundabout and through the next with the entrance to PENCLACWYDD wild foul centre on your left, after passing TROSTRE steel works at the next roundabout watch for the sign on exit to MACHYNYS, CARMARTHEN Coastal Road. Drive along until you arrive at the signpost at MACHYNYS/CARMARTHEN B4304, just after this sign is a roundabout with large boulders/rocks in the middle, turn left here down on a unmade road to fish two venues. Training Wall & Firing Range.

(NB: Access difficult at this time ongoing construction work)

Machynys Gully, in front of firing range. Penclawdd in the Background.

Training Wall – tide out.

Venue 1: Bottom Water – Training Wall (NGR 49.8/97.4)

Park the car at the top of the slipway with the "Training Wall" entrance marker pole in front of you some 700 yards distant.

There is some element of danger fishing this venue, so take care.

Walk out across the sand heading towards the channel guidance post, then out to the rocks walking to the end to fish alongside the post, casting towards the rocks of CROFTY.

If this is the first time at this venue only fish one hour into the in coming tide because the tide WILL cut you off, coming behind you through the breaks in the rocks, so check the time of the tide and be very very wary, experience will allow you to fish longer, but watch the tide and do not fish alone.

Try using a single hook flowing trace up to 4 foot in length for Bass. Expect some tackle losses in amongst the swirling pools.

Venue 2: Rifle Range – Top Water (NGR 51.6/97.4)

To fish the firing range rather than park the car up the slipway carry on down the unmade road to "MACHYNYS POOLS" on your left, and the derelict rifle range structure in front of you, park at this point. Cross over the wall and walk straight down to the estuary on the incoming tide to fish all the way in along the gully between CARREG FACH *(SMALL STONE)* and CARREG DDU *(BLACK STONE)*. Still in danger of being cut off by the incoming tide out on the mud flats, so take care.

Fish between the deep gully and the wooden posted groyne at top water.

Species: BASS, FLOUNDER, MULLET, EELS.

The original bridge to cross the Burry Estuary opened on the 7th June 1834, and virtually rebuilt in 1862. Most of the timber beams in the 700 Foot long bridge being replaced by iron girders which had been made in LLANELLI.

A gentleman by the name of Mr Mc KIERON of BURRY PORT was in charge of the rebuilding. It opened on the 26th April, 1923 at a cost of £70,000.

The present bridge was built alongside and opened on the 9th August, 1988 at a cost of £7,000,000. All that is left of the old bridge are the wooden stumps.

Footnote: At this time July, 2004, because of a Millennium project on going with the building of a Golf course on the "MACHYNYS PENINSULA" a difficult venue to reach.

Llanelli – North Dock

Camping/Caravans	No
Disabled	No
Bait	Blow Lugworm, Cockle
Seafood	Cockle

Directions

From the Severn bridge area come off the M4 motorway at junction 47, take the A 483 towards Swansea, at the next roundabout turn right on the A484 towards LLANELLI. Follow the A484 across the estuary road bridge, straight on until you pass TROSTRE steelworks then at the next roundabout watch for the sign on exit for MACHYNYS CARMARTHEN Coastal Road B4304, carry straight on passing "COPPERHOUSE" roundabout, then turn left at "LLEIDI" roundabout, sign posted North Dock and beach. Over two small bridges then first left with the river LLEIDI running beneath and over the second. On your right hand side is the area where the LLANELLI tide table readings are taken.

Drive around to park at the foreshore near the café *(under threat of closure)* nice clean seaside café serving in car type food *(More construction work ongoing).*

Tree that was planted outside the Millennium Office at North Dock, Llanelli.

Open wind swept beach with the wind coming up the Burry estuary, in the distance is WHITFORD LIGHTHOUSE, the only cast iron lighthouse in the country, at this time derelict – can lottery money bring it back to life?

Water colour plays an important role when fishing LLANELLI beach as it does all around the Pembrokeshire coastline, so use a number of fluorescent beads if the water is discoloured on paternoster type rigs for Flounder and Bass.

Try a mixture of baits, Lugworm, Crab tipped with Lugworm, harbour Ragworm, try it tipped with a strip of Mackerel.

Top water venue all along this stretch of coastline, the Burry inlet virtually empties on every tide.

Venue 1: (NGR 49.6/99.3)

Walk to the left of the wall and fish between here and the new rock groyne structure.

A mixture of sand and shingle at top water, sand/mud bottom water.

Venue 2: (NGR 50.2/98.7)

North Dock, Llanelli, where the tide tables are taken from.

From the car park head back towards MACHYNYS to your left some nine hundred yards to fish the small bay where the river LLEDI meets up with the river DAFEN.

Footnote: It was reported that a eight foot STURGEON was caught at this mark in a pool at low water on the 12th of October 1806.

In the first week of June 2004, another eight foot STURGEON (called STANLEY) was caught roughly along the same stretch of coastline, almost 200 YEARS later.

Venue 3: (NGR 49.3/00.3)

Parking: Instead of turning left at North Dock sign, carry straight on and take the next left before the MILLENNIUM project office *(A millennium tree was planted here on the 7th of September 1997)* walk to the railway crossing bridge which allows access to "SANDY WATER PARK", and fish the small bay near the rocks, passed the railway bridge there are large boulders positioned at the top water mark.

NB: be wary if digging lugworm, the tide sweeps up the river past PWLL on your right.

The DAFEN river bridge at "COPPERHOUSE" roundabout was opened on the 22nd February, 1993 and the two rivers of the LLEIDI and DAFEN meet up at this point. As you cross the road bridge coming from the Swansea area, on the right hand side is a small brick building to operate the hydraulic sluice gate that releases the water out of the DAFEN river LAGOON into the sea.

For a couple of hours top water fishing, park here, cross the road and fish off the flat concrete wall type platform.

Footnote: The first canned beer in Britain was made at FELINFOEL, LLANELLI on December the 3rd 1935.

Pwll

Camping/Caravans	No
Disabled	No
Bait	Blow Lugworm, limited Crab, Mussel
Seafood	Mussel

Directions

Come off the M4 motorway at junction 47 take the A483 towards Swansea, at the next roundabout turn right onto the A484 towards LLANELLI. Follow the A484 across the LOUGHOR estuary road bridge, and after passing TROSTRE steelworks watch for the sign on exit of the roundabout for MACHYNYS/CARMARTHEN coastal road B4304. Straight on at "COPPERHOUSE" roundabout, through "LLEIDI" roundabout CARMARTHEN B4304, and at "SEASIDE" roundabout bare left over the railway bridge still on the B4304 and then at "SANDY" roundabout you will be coming off the B4304 back onto the A484 towards Burry Port. Drive onto the PWLL sign opposite the CARMARTHENSHIRE college campus, park on the road just after the PWLL sign, just before a closed down garage, walk down the lane for some 400 yards to the railway track.

Llanelli Beach.

14

After crossing the railway line go down the slippery giant man made steps to the really muddy foreshore – three inches of mud for twenty yards or so then peat and Mussel beds to the "BARNABY" pill at bottom water. To the right, about two hundred yards away you will come to a river tumbling out into the pill, its exit onto the beach is covered by a steel grid and a thick sheet of rubber to act as a non return valve, to try to prevent the surrounding fields from becoming flooded by the incoming tide. Although a muddy venue can be quite productive on occasions with some nice flounder.

Looking towards Pwll from Llanelli beach.

Venue 1: (NGR 48.5/00.4)

When you arrive at the bottom of the steps trudge your way through the mud for some hundred yards left and behind you at this point is a 'W' warning sign for the train, and in front of you the edge of the Mussel beds, visible at low water.

Fish a 6.5 metre type tide, LLANELLI tide table, on the incoming tide, and a couple of hours on the ebb.

Use a trace with the hooks above the lead with a number of 5mm beads and sequins, even a couple of floating beads to help keep the bait out of the mud.

Fishing is best later on in the year after the first frost when the crab are less troublesome.

Lugworm visible at bottom water. Some caution required.

If you like fishing and sloshing around in the mud this is the venue for you.

15

Burry Port

Camping/Caravans	Yes, shoreline
Disabled	Yes, with some help
Bait	Crab past the black pipe, Mussel, lugworm
Seafood	Mussel

Directions

From the CARDIFF area come off the M4 motorway at junction 47, take the A483 towards SWANSEA, at the next roundabout turn right on to the A484 towards LLANELLI. Follow the A484 over the estuary road bridge and after passing TROSTRE steel works at the next roundabout watch for the sign on exit for MACHYNYS – CARMARTHEN coastal road B4304, then drive on passing "COPPERHOUSE, LLEIDI and SEASIDE" roundabouts then at "SANDY" roundabout come off the B4304 back onto the A484 driving through PWLL towards BURRY PORT.

Turn left at the town centre sign B4311 BURRY PORT down through the town centre left over the railway bridge CARMARTHEN B4311, then left at the harbour and caravan site "SHORELINE" Caravan park, to park at the harbour mouth by BURRY PORT yacht club west pier.

To fish the east pier instead of driving through the town centre drive straight down CHURCH ROAD across the railway line and following the road around to the life boat station. Drive up onto the top road to the left for about three hundred yards or so to park near the small boat launching slipway.

2003 car parking charges:
WEST PIER £1.00 for two hours. EAST PIER £3.00 all day.

But there is an alternative, when you cross the railway track turn sharp left and follow the road around through a small industrial estate to park free at the end of the cycle track, near BLACK SCAR rocks. *(You could have dropped passengers near the venue of your choice because West Pier is a good walk from this point).*

Venue 1: West Dock Pier (NGR 44.5/99.9)

Walk out along the pier past the lighthouse to fish off the end eastwards towards top water. Then as the tide is on the wane and for some shelter out of the wind, fish on the right hand side of the lighthouse behind the wall on the stone slope into the pill.

Along the whole stretch of coast line the tide goes out a long way, just the river outlets left at bottom water. *NB: Be a bit wary whilst digging lugworm.*

The old PEMBREY HARBOUR PILL starts 600 yards westward, snaking its way up through a series of "S" bends through BURRY PORT meeting up with the "BARNABY PILL" at PWLL, to continue past LLANELLI beach up to MACHYNYS.

Venue 2: East Pier and Lifeboat Station (NGR 44.8/00.2)

Fishing towards top water, fish off the small slipway or just to the left of a small concrete ramp like structure, to fish the first run of the tide, after the slipway walk to the apex of the sea defence wall to fish for WHITING and small CODLING winter months, BASS, MULLET and FLOUNDER summer months.

Burry Port harbour.

Behind you at this time are the remains of the "BURRY PORT POWER STATION" with the black intake pipe still visible going out to sea, the outlet pipe from the station has disintegrated by the power of the tides. When the power station, now long gone, was in operation the water from the discharge pipe was of a very small higher temperature, and used to be a popular feeding ground for BASS and MULLET.

Another venue 50 or so yards passed the black pipe is a black scar of rocks, to fish for BASS first run of the tide into the gully. Very rocky area so use rotten bottom traces, tackle losses could be high.

Footnote: On the 18th June, 1928 an American seaplane called "FRIENDSHIP" landed between PWLL and the Black pipe area of BURRY PORT.

On board where Commander STULZ, co-pilot MISS AMELIA EARHART, the first woman to fly the Atlantic and Mechanic LOU GORDON, they flew from TREPASSEY BAY, NEWFOUNDLAND to BURRY PORT, the flight took 20 hours and 49 minutes.

The "GEORGE" hotel in BURRY PORT has an excellent collection of AMELIA EARHART memorabilia.

Taken from the old Burry Port harbour, looking towards the lighthouse.

18

Cefn Sidan (Silken Ridge)

Camping/Caravans	By arrangement. Ring Pembrey Country Park: 01554 833913
Disabled	No
Bait	Black Lugworm, some Razor Fish, Cockles, Mussels, Whelks.
Seafood	Mussels, Razor Fish, Cockles, Whelks.

Directions

From the Severn bridge direction come off the M4 motorway at junction 47, take A483 towards Swansea, at the next roundabout turn right onto the A484 towards LLANELLI. Follow the A484 over the estuary road bridge and after passing TROSTRE steelworks at the next roundabout watch for the sign on exit for MACHYNYS – CARMARTHEN coastal road B4304. Follow the road until you reach "SANDY" roundabout (sign posted) then go back onto the A484 towards BURRY PORT.

After BURRY PORT it's a further 2 miles to the PEMBREY country park sign, turn left at this point over the railway bridge down the marshland road, then take the first left after the concrete wartime lookout bunker, follow the narrow road to the left of the brick building (do not drive into the country park), drive along the narrow tarmacadam road as far as possible to the free car park (DEBTORS ROAD). It is possible to drive on to the beach over the dunes at this point with a four wheel drive vehicle, but I suggest you walk the 400 yards over the dunes before contemplating taking a chance, but if you do decide to chance it leave some air out of the tyres, look at the return trip.

Wreck of the 'Paul' at the entrance of the river Gwendraeth, Cefn Sidan.

Venue 1: "Pool" (NGR 40.6/99.4)

When you emerge onto the beach at the red and white striped post walk straight down for some 300 yards and try to arrive about two hours after bottom water

When I began researching this book the tide would come up the small channel to form a pool towards the top water mark and then sweep away to your left, but now because of the sand dredging this pool has disappeared. About two hours before top water has been the most productive for me but this could all change.

Facing you over the sea at this point, is WORMS HEAD and CEFN BRYN, on the GOWER coast.

Footnote: On the 17th May 1934 a "MERMAID!" was supposed to be seen in this pool,

Venue 2: "Teviotdale" (NGR 37.8/01.6)

It would help if a four wheel drive vehicle is available to get you from the car park across the dunes onto the beach as the bait diggers do, heading for the wreck of the "TEVIOTDALE" a four masted iron sailing ship wrecked on the 15th October, 1886. The jumble of boulders at the top of the beach is approximately one and three quarters miles from the car park. To fish the venue to commence at bottom water, carry on past the jumble of boulders and the wooden remains of a further two wrecks, then head down to the sea by the 15 concrete remains of a small upright wreck structure with Mussel attached.

Venue 3: Near the wreck of the "Craigwhinnie" (NGR 35.7/04.2)

Fish the gully in front of the control tower as the tide is coming through. *(NB: The RAF do low flying exercises and firing in this area, but there is no flying at this time on Saturday and Sunday.)* On your right on the sand bar is the wreck of the "CRAIGWHINNIE". A IRON BARQUE wrecked on the 19th November, 1899 or the 20th December, 1899, further along the coast at TYWYN POINT are the remains of the

"TYWYN" wooden DZ structure, with Mussel attached to the framework, also discarded bullet shells.

Further along is the wreck of the "PAUL" a German four masted schooner built in Seattle America between 1914 and 1918, stranded at this point on the 30th October, 1925.

You are approximately 6 miles from the car park.

CEFN SIDAN, so called because a vessel with silk on board was wrecked on this stretch.

NB: At the exit onto the beach from PEMBREY country park are five life saving buoys, situated at top water spaced 200 yards apart, one at the exit two to the left and two to the right. Some caution is required if swimming in this area at bottom water, FAST tidal run.

Baits: *BLACK LUGWORM* at present, but how long will they last with the amount of bait diggers?

Main quarry SEA BASS.

The Towyn DZ Pontoon at Cefn Sidan beach. There are Mussels stuck to the stantions and a mixture of bullet shells in the water. Look-out tower in the background.

Kidwelly – Gwendraeth Fach

Camping/Caravans	No
Disabled	No
Bait	No
Seafood	No

Kidwelly Castle.

Directions

From PEMBREY carry on the A484 until you come to "PONTYRHYD" roundabout, turn left and drive into KIDWELLY. Turn left at the station sign opposite the "FISHERMANS ARMS" public house, travel along Station Road over the railway track, then take the right hand fork along a narrow road, there will be a small sewerage works on your left hand side. Park at the small Quay car park.

I mention this venue only in reference to you having possibly an hour or two to spare on your holidays, and after visiting the castle perhaps a trip to the GWENDRAETH river picnic area, for a cast or two to practice some casting or to iron out any reel problems, top water only. If you attempt to fish really tough baits only, loads of crab in the river.

DO NOT venture out onto the marsh lands DEEP MUD.

There is a chip shop next to the FISHERMANS ARMS public house.

Kidwelly Quay – the railway bridge crossing over the river Gwendraeth.

Carmarthen Bay

Camping/Caravans	Statics and Chalets only
Disabled	No
Bait	Blow and black lugworm, crab, mussel, cockle, ragworm.
Seafood	mussel and cockle.

Directions

Come off the M4 motorway at junction 47, take the A483 towards Swansea, at the next roundabout turn right on the A484 towards LLANELLI. Follow the A484 over the estuary road bridge and after passing TROSTRE steelworks watch for the sign on exit for MACHYNYS – CARMARTHEN coastal road B4304. Follow this road until your reach "SANDY" roundabout then go back onto the A484 towards BURRY PORT. At the BURRY PORT sign its 4.8 miles until you reach "PONTYRHYD" roundabout, turn left into KIDWELLY and after crossing the bridge with the GWENDRAETH river running beneath, look for the sign to turn left FERRYSIDE 3 miles, down a narrow road then left at the sign CARMARTHEN BAY HOLIDAY CENTRE *(A Haven site at present).*

Holiday park sign posted, drive down across the railway track and travel towards the end of the site towards ST. ISMAELS to park above a sandy bay.

CARMARTHEN BAY: Holiday park telephone number 01267 267511.

Venue 1: Stephens Bay (NGR 37.5/07.0)

There is a fast tidal run up the GWENDRAETH channel past the holiday village. If it is your first time at this venue try on a low tide *(NEAP)* as soon as it starts to make, slightly to the left of alignment of the car between the rocks and the bay in front of the car. Avoiding the small boats mooring ropes towards the outcrop of Black Scar rocks, in to the GWENDRAETH GULLY for Bass and Flounder.

Its approximately half a mile to bottom water to collect soft and peeler crab in season amongst the stones.

COCKLES: From the car straight down a couple of hundred yards then slightly to the right.

LUGWORM: Straight down.

BLACK LUGWORM: Will have to search out, the beds keep changing.

Popular holiday resort, so fish for BASS, FLOUNDER, MULLET, early morning, towards dusk, or inclement weather.

Carmarthen Bay Holiday Village at bottom water.

St. Ismaels

Camping/Caravans	No
Disabled	No
Bait	Lugworm, Crab, Mussel, Cockle.
Seafood	Mussel, Cockle.

Directions

Carrying on from the sign to CARMARTHEN BAY holiday village – its 1.3 miles to the white railway crossing gates of ST. ISMAELS, just before the parish church.

This is the bottom road to FERRYSIDE from KIDWELLY.

Park the car by the gates and cross the railway track (watch for the train) to the remains of an old wartime lookout post.

Footnote: The river TOWY *(AFON TYWI)* is finally reaching the sea after travelling some 70 miles from its source in the Cambrian mountains, making its way out between CEFN SIDAN and LAUGHARNE sands.

The rocky foreshore of St. Ismaels, near Ferryside.

The wartime look-out post at St. Ismaels.

Venue 1: Look-Out Post (NGR 36.3/07.7)

I mention this venue in respect of only gathering some bait, its such a flat section of bay that when the tide decides to make it comes in at a rate of knots, better to carry on to FERRYSIDE to fish off "BIG BEN ROCK".

Some excellent cockles can be raked up in front of the look out post just clear of the stones, but take care watch the tide if cockling or fishing.

Ferryside

Camping/Caravans	Statics only at POACHERS REST
Disabled	Possible top water only yacht club
Bait	Blow and Black worm, limited Crab
Seafood	No

Directions

From the SEVERN BRIDGE/CARDIFF areas come off the M4 motorway at junction 47, take the A483 towards SWANSEA. At the next roundabout turn right onto the A484 towards LLANELLI, follow the A484 over the estuary road bridge straight on to the next roundabout and after passing TROSTRE steelworks, at the next roundabout take the MACHYNYS/CARMARTHEN coastal road B4304, follow this road until you reach "SANDY" roundabout then go back on to the A484 towards BURRY PORT. Carry on for 4.8 miles until you reach "PONTYRHYD" *(PONT-HER-REED)* roundabout, turn left into KIDWELLY, as you drive through the village watch for the FERRYSIDE sign, turn left at FERRY ROAD towards CARMARTHEN BAY holiday village then take the right hand road sign posted to LLANSAINT and FERRYSIDE 3 miles. This is the top road to FERRYSIDE. Bottom road see ST. ISMAELS.

At FERRYSIDE, drive across the railway track and park by the yacht club.

Looking across the estuary at Ferryside from Llansteffan Castle.

Venue 1: Yacht Club (NGR 36.5/10.4)

There is a channel guidance post some 450 yards to the left of the yacht club, and behind you at this point is a house with a red roof tiles and spire, there are patches of sticky mud along this stretch of bay, so fish to the left onto firmer sand, strange venue to fish because the fish will sometimes come towards top water or when the tide is nearly down to the river TOWY. So whatever the state of tide when you arrive it might still produce.

The tide will flood to your left forcing you back to the rocks at top water.

Venue 2: "Yellow Post" (NGR 37.0/11.2)

When you arrive at FERRYSIDE with the railway station in front of you, turn right down passed the school and rugby club, over a small bridge and turn sharp left down a narrow road for half a mile or so to park in a very small lay by, difficult to turn the car by BRONYN FARM.

Go across the railway track and along the sand bar on the right hand side for a little over half a mile from the car, to fish opposite LLANSTEFFAN yacht club (you can see the boats across the river TOWY) by the yellow post, two hours from top water, no need to cross "ROTTON PILLS" really sticky mud, and watch the height of the tide as it does flood the marsh – ASK.

Footnote: If you decide to walk up the railway track to fish higher up the TOWY be careful the railway police do not take kindly to this practice, but there is a nice venue after the railway bridge across a field to fish off the banks, with some shelter amongst the bushes and trees, worth a try.

Venue 3: "Big Ben Rock" or "Red Rock" (NGR 36.5/10.3)

Turn left this time before the railway station down HOLCWM way passing the village hall, at the entrance to POACHERS REST there is a small public footpath to the beach on the right hand side, when you are on the railway track look to the left BIG BEN ROCK is some 600 yards distant in the direction of ST.ISMAELS. Scramble up on top of

BIG BEN to fish off the red flat stone / rock platform, casting over the rocks which are only for some 15 yards then on to cleaner sand.

Limited fishing at top water.

To Summarise: At FERRYSIDE the tide seems to go out for ever, two hours after bottom water the river TOWY is still emptying into the sea with just the tributaries making gullies into the river, but when the tide eventually starts to make it rushes in, so be sensible and pick a middle height tide when the flood is not so fierce. But I must again stress take care out on the marshlands.

JULY/AUGUST with crab BASS/FLOUNDER.

Static caravans at POACHERS REST, some for hire.

Tourers at TANLAN, CARMARTHEN BAY. Telephone number Ferryside 267306, booking in at the farm opposite the duck pond, limited facilities.

'Big Ben' rock, between St. Ismaels and Ferryside.

Llansteffan

Camping/Caravans	SUNRISE BAY
Disabled	No
Bait	Limited Blow Lugworm/Crab/Mussel
Seafood	No

Directions

When you arrive at CARMARTHEN from the SEVERN BRIDGE or surrounding areas, straight on at the first roundabout, left at the next, A40 to ST. CLEARS, then first left after the bridge onto the B4312 to LLANSTEFFAN, a distance of seven miles from the CARMARTHEN round about. Driving down through JOHNSTOWN/LLANGAIN, with the river TOWY on your left, and on to LLANSTEFFAN.

Turn left at the sign to the beach and park at the end of the "GREEN" by the mobile fish and chip cabin. Fresh drinking water by the cabin, toilet facilities and telephone by the entrance to the car park.

Footnote: There are some excellent views from the NORMAN castle over the river "TAF" and "TOWY" estuaries, and across the bay to FERRYSIDE.

Scotts Bay, Llansteffan and St. Anthony's Cottage.

Venue 1: "Scots Bay" (NGR 34.9/09.9)

There are a couple of marks to fish along this stretch of sandy coastline, bottom water in front of the car park, the rocks below the ruined look out NORMAN CASTLE arrow tower. But let us go across to SCOTTS BAY to fish off the rocks by the escape route steps near ST. ANTONYS cottage.

After parking walk out past the small playground to the right in plenty of time before the tide cuts your access along the beach, passing the first set of steps up off the beach, continue until you reach the second set of escape route steps.

You need a reasonably high tide to have any depth of water. Fish the flat rock section at top water near the hand-railing, casting into the mouth of the river TOWY. Take care with the waves coming over the rocks.

Fishes best after a blow out to sea, when the water is not so clear. Lugworm can be dug but not easy from the bottom water mark up. Limited amount of crab and cockle around WHARLEY point and the guidance post Scotts Bay at bottom water. A nice woodland path to Scotts Bay, the walk begins just to the left of the path up to the castle.

Footnote: There is a medieval shrine called ST. ANTONYS WELL situated at Scotts Bay, ninety yards up the path to right of the house on the beach ST. ANTONYS cottage, above the arched doorway are the words FFYNNON *(WELL)* ANTWN *(ANTONY)* SANT *(SAINT)* through the doorway down some steps to the well, small square enclosure known as a rushing well although there is only a trickle of water inside the shrine at present, the main stream runs outside and out on to Scotts Bay worth a look.

Wharley Point

Venue 2: Waterfall Bay (NGR 33.4/09.5)

To fish below WHARLEY POINT (Height 360 feet) at LLAN-STEFFAN instead of turning left for the beach, carry straight on up the hill past the school and the STICKS HOTEL, follow the sign for LLANYBRI until you come to a bend in the road and sign posted

LLANYBRI and CHESHIRE HOMES take the left hand road not sign posted down along this road until you reach a wooden sign on the left hand side NATIONAL TRUST and "LORDS PARK FARM" turn left here for 4/10ths of a mile to a small lay by on the left hand side covered with chippings. The steel gate is opposite for access down to "WATERFALL BAY" also known as "COVER CLIFT" or the "GASH".

The farmer allows access to the bay, but please close the gate, no litter – no dogs, livestock grazing. Pass through the gate down a grass bank with access to the beach via a series of ropes down through a small waterfall if there has been a lot of rain. Distance from the car some 400 yards.

When you get down walk to the right approximately 300 yards to the edge of the stones to fish the river TAF on the incoming tide in front of WHARLEY HILL.

Fish low to middle height tides because of the fast tidal run up the river TAF arrive two hours after bottom water to fish for BASS-FLOUNDER-GOLDEN and GREY MULLET.

Baits: Peeler and Soft Crab in season – Great large Mussels some with small crab living inside.

Very limited amount of Blow Lugworm. So take bait down with you.

Crab and Black Lugworm for Bass-Harbour Ragworm for Flounder and Mullet.

Rigs: PATERNOSTER, PULLY, PENNEL, DOUBLE PATTING.

NB: Again some caution required at this venue, opposite is GINST POINT.

Footnote: A couple of hundred yards past the lay by car park is a small wooden sign to "WHARLEY POINT" for some stunning views over Ginst Point with the outlets from "RAILSGATE PILL" making its way to the river TAF across LAUGHARNE sands and the Cockle Beds.

Llanybri

Camping/Caravans	No
Disabled	No
Bait	No
Seafood	No

Directions

Arriving at CARMARTHEN, straight on at the first roundabout left at the next, A40 towards ST. CLEARS, then it's the first left after the bridge onto the B4312 to LLANSTEFFAN. Driving through JOHNSTOWN then LLANGAIN, the river TOWY will be on your left. When you arrive at the beach sign in LLANSTEFFAN carry straight on past the "STICKS HOTEL" for a distance of 1.7 miles to a small crossroads at LLANYBRI. Drive straight across passing a farm on your left, then turn left at "LLANYBRI HOUSE" down a steep hill and over a small bridge, then next left down a narrow road straight on at the dead end sign to park at "CWM CELYN" farm, a distance of 3.2 miles from the beach sign at LLANSTEFFAN.

There is a small car parking fee, do not park and obstruct farm machinery.

I am very wary/cautious at this venue because the marsh area is so flat. So check with your tide table, low tides only, especially to start.

Cwm Celyn Farm, Llanybri.
Pay here and ask for advice.

Venue 1: River Taf (NGR 31.6/12.3)

Walk out across the marsh grass to arrive at the rivers edge at bottom water to pick out your spot before the tide eventually decides to make, look for the small river channel outlets, the likely flounder feeding grounds.

Flounder are spent early on in the year, and crab likely to be troublesome. Nice flounder during the winter months, and especially after the first frosts.

Try harbour ragworm tipped with a tiny piece of MACKEREL or BLACK LUGWORM, for a early spring BASS.

NB: This venue is only for low tide fishing, the marsh will get flooded on a high tide, so take care if you are unsure or if it is your first time at this venue, ask at the farmhouse or when paying for parking.

DO NOT TAKE RISKS

Llanybri marshes, low tide venue. Extreme care required.

Laugharne

Camping/Caravans	Ants Hill
Disabled	Yes: Venue 1
Bait	Poor Ragworm. Limited Crab
Seafood	Some Samphire in season

Directions

At the second roundabout at CARMARTHEN take the A40 ST. CLEARS road, drive on until you see the sign PENDINE A4066, then after the bridge take the slip road sign posted ST. CLEARS – LAUGHARNE A4066, then right again sign posted LAUGHARNE – which is four miles distant. Driving through ST. CLEARS over a small bridge with the upper reaches of the river TAF beneath, on past a nine hole golf course on your left, (watch for the sign HALFPENNY FURSE) and so on to LAUGHARRNE to park in the free castle car park. On a very high tide the car park is liable to flooding with the tide winding its way up the "CORRAN" stream.

There is a small brick pumping station on the left hand side just before the stream, a drinking water tap is located at this point.

Upstream Dylan's Pill, Laugharne.

Venue 1: Boat House (NGR 30.6/11.0)

Cross over the small bridge with the "CORRAN" stream running beneath with the castle on your left, along a rough path then onto a paved path. Follow this to the end to begin fishing some three and a half hours before top water.

Samphire at Laugharne.

Comfortable fishing you can sit on the wall. Crab troublesome during the summer months, so try some of the tougher baits: SQUID, MACKEREL, RAGWORM tipped with a piece of limpet or the best of all SOFT and PEELER CRAB.

Winter months best at LAUGHARNE. Species, BASS-FLOUNDER, and some MULLET on occasions.

Venue 2: Dylans Pill (NGR 30.9/11.5)

When you arrive at LLAUGHARNE turn left after "BROWNS HOTEL" *(was popular with the poet DYLAN THOMAS, buried in the local churchyard)* sign posted LAUGHARNE PARK, drive through "SEASONS" at this time – time share holiday village passing "CATLINS" restaurant and clubhouse, to park on the flat wooded area, do not take the car down to the beach, lock out posts on the hill.

After parking walk down the steep driveway, then turn left at the slipway walk for a couple of hundred yards to the end of the trees to fish "DYLANS PILL" beneath "GIN HILL". Look for the stone seat built into the rock face to make camp during inclement weather, nice sandy area at top water with trees at your back for shelter. Use a light rod for a bit of close range fun fishing.

The river TAF comes in running north eastwards, to commence fishing depending on the height of the tide about three and a half hours before top water.

Venue 3: Barks Bay (NGR 30.5/10.5)

To fish BARKS leave the car at the castle car park and walk along the strand, passing the small sewerage treatment plant on your right, walk out on to the mud flats and turn right towards "MAINSTONE". The big yellow top rock. This is the least fished venue at LAUGHARNE because its muddy and the fast run up the gully of the river TAF towards you from GINST POINT, but it is well worth a try first run of the tide.

It is possible on a low tide to fish the tide all the way in at this mark fishing off "FLAT ROCK", it is the flat seaweed covered rock with the fallen tree *(if it is still there after publishing)* at your back. If your escape route looks like being cut off, retreat back to the bend in front of the sewerage works to fish the eddies close range.

Some poor ragworm can be dug at low water near "MAINSTONE" on the flat shingle/mud bank, also near the sewerage outfall marker pole.

Limited crab at "MAINSTONE". Hopefully the SAMPHIRE WEED will still be there in season alongside the concrete covered outfall pipe.

Venue 4: Railsgate Pill (NGR 30.3/09.7)

ONLY OF INTEREST: Walk along the strand, and before the small sewerage treatment plant just before the seat is the path sign posted to go up through "SIR JOHNS HILL" *(SURGEON HILL)* follow the path until you reach the CARMARTHEN BAY coastal sign, go down the hill and man made steps covered in wild strawberries and you will reach "QUAY BRIDGE", and a simple one way plate valve system that has enabled acres of marshland to be reclaimed.

Because the tide is unable to travel further than QUAY BRIDGE it has cut numerous gullies and small tributaries which flow out across LAUGHARNE sands to GINST POINT

To the side of the bridge is a small muddy QUAY where the small boats where tied up to load the limestone to travel the short journey to LAUGHARNE LIME KILN on the strand, now sadly gone to build a wall.

There are some SMALL ragworm in the MUDDY gullies but please DO NOT be tempted to dig, EXTREMELY deep mud and some danger
SO TAKE CARE

Footnote: Does the TAF rise at a peak at the top of the PRESELI MOUNTAINS called BRENIN FAWR *(GREAT KING)* some fifteen or sixteen miles to the north of LAUGHARNE?

Ginst Point

Camping/Caravans	Nine Acres
Disabled	No
Bait	Very limited Cockle, Lugwrom, Crab
Seafood	Cockle

Directions

From the CARDIFF/SEVERN BRIDGE areas take the M4 motorway to CARMARTHEN, turn left at the second roundabout A40, ST. CLEARS, continue on this road until you see the sign LAUGHARNE/PENDINE A4066, its left after the road bridge.

After passing through LAUGHARNE and BROADWAY and a small caravan park on the right watch for a sign on a farm gate "KYNGADLE FARM", take the next left opposite "HILL CREST" bungalow down the causeway marsh road passing "NINE ACRES" caravan park, and on to the Ministry of Defence land. There is a restricted area to the right of the gate so bare left and follow the narrow road for two miles to park in the sanded/grass car park by E7 WATCH TOWER.

Looking from St. John's Wood, one of the exit points to Railsgate Pill, with Ginst Point in the background.

39

NB: *There is a mid week time restriction on to the Ministry of Defence land, open on most weekends, but owing to problems throughout our world the armed forces could be on alert and access will be denied. So call first to make sure the beach will be open. Telephone number M.O.D. Police: 01994 452310.*

Venue 1: Ginst Point (NGR 33.6/08.7)

Cross the small bank and walk left *(eastwards)* for half a mile, as you walk towards WHARLEY POINT. On the other side of the river TAF you will be passing on your left an outlet strange gully from RAILSGATE PILL where the tide will make towards top water *(Venue 2).* This is one of the many outlets from RAILSGATE, do not be tempted to cross the pill when the tide is making, you will be isolated out on the sand bar.

After approximately half a mile you reach the flat muddy sand area with a small stream running left to right, fish at this point. It takes some time for the tide to make so a couple of hours after bottom water will be ok on about a 5.7 metre tide, the higher the tide the sooner you will be fishing Venue 2. Try and fish into the turbulence caused by the outgoing river and the incoming tide as long as possible. – Cockles along this section of beach.

Railsgate Pill near Ginst Point, from Wharley Hill.

To your left runs the river TAF across the bay the river TOWY, and the GWENDRAETH. The three rivers look like a crows foot on the map.

We have a BASS nursery area from GINST POINT across the bay to the right of the GWENDRAETH to TYWYN POINT with boat and netting restrictions from the 1st of May until the 31st of October.

Venue 2: Railsgate Pill (NGR 32.9/08.7)

When the tide forces you from the point, make a steady retreat fishing into the pill as it curves around in front of the grassed marshland.

Venue 3: E7 Look-Out Tower (NGR 32.0/07.8)

Top Water Venue: After parking walk straight out down the slipway to the corner of the big jumble of rocks to fish just to the left. If the water is gin clear try a simple trace without beads, but after a blow out to sea and the water is discoloured try a number of 5mm green and black beads.

Traces: Just a suggestion. Running Paternoster, Wired Paternoster, Pennell-Pully *(See trace drawings).* Double Patting, which means a spare trace ready baited up hanging on the rod rest.

Take the bait of your choice down with you.

Species: BASS, FLOUNDER, MULLET and some SILVER EEL.

Footnote: TWIN TOWERS See PENDINE Bottom Water Walk.
If you decide to have a walk to the towers its approximately two miles westwards from GINST. About half a mile into the walk you come to an old steel structure wreck that I believe to be of the "FRANCIS BEDDOE" sunk 1920. And then on into the "PENDINE TRIANGLE" with its warning and keep out signs, there are numerous discarded empty rocket shells along the beach, especially at the top water mark Its amazing how much plastic rubbish is trapped along this stretch of coastline.

In front of TWIN TOWERS towards bottom water are the wooden remains of an old fish trap system.

Pendine

Camping/Caravans	Mainly Statics
Disabled	YES: Not easy, but if able, try by the "CLIFF" Snack Bar early season, and when the holiday season is nearing the end, much quieter and more enjoyable. There is a small wall that you have to cast over. Try casting just to the edge of the rocks on to clean sand. Fish towards top water on the higher tides.
Bait	Lugworm, limited Crab, small mussel, venus shells
Seafood	Laver Weed (Laverbread), Winkles, Cockles

Directions

From the direction of CARDIFF take the M4 Motorway to CARMARTHEN, straight on at the first roundabout, left at the second A40 to ST. CLEARS (You now have 18.5 miles to go to PENDINE). Turn left after travelling under the third road bridge A4066 sign posted LAUGHARNE & PENDINE. Drive through LAUGHARNE BROOK, LLANMILOE and so to PENDINE.

By the "BEACH HOTEL" there is parking space for cars displaying a disabled badge, and just enough room for another two cars. Two public houses in PENDINE "The BEACH HOTEL" and the "SPRINGWELL".

As strange as it sounds if you decide to take your car onto the beach during the summer months there is a parking fee! But anyway, if you do, drive along the hard sand at the top water mark to "TWIN TOWERS" and leave it at the top of the beach and walk down to fish.

Pendine.

Venue 1: Look-Out Tower and Twin Towers (NGR 28.5/05.8)

To the left of the beach, mainly an evening or weekend venue, because some 500 yards distant is a Ministry of Defence PROOF AND EXPERIMENTAL ESTABLISHMENT warning notice, and when the red flag is flying entry to this stretch of beach is prohibited.

A long walk to the look out tower two miles and a further three quarters of a mile to TWIN TOWERS, and a full three miles to the gully/sand bar at bottom water (NGR 27.5/08.7). The sand is firm at the top of the beach to enable you to drive to the venue. *NB: Sand is soft middle to bottom water.*

To the left of TWIN TOWERS at bottom water is a gully with a sand bar in the bay, try here in to the gully for BASS but at this moment in time late 2003 a little sparce.

Walk the beach at bottom water, looking for flounder marks (they are circular indent rings in the sand and you can see the additional rings as they swim free on the outgoing tide).

Venue 2: Well Beach (NGR 23.4/07.5)

In front of the BEACH HOTEL, start fishing at this venue one and a half hours before bottom water. Fish in shorts summer months, chest waders later on in the year, reason being long casts required on the outgoing tide, but at top water no need to cast any distance. Fishing will be slow, so if tidal conditions allow use two rods – double patting and move along the beach.

Reels: Whatever type is your preference, multyplier or fixed spool, but make sure the spool is large enough to hold sufficient line.

Venue 3: between Dolwen Point and Gilman Point (NGR 23.2/07.5)

Unsuitable fishing at GILMAN POINT at top water – very rocky. Limited amount of Peeler and Soft Crab amongst the rocks near DOLWEN POINT. And a little amount of Laver Weed.

NB: This is a cut off venue at top water, but there is a escape route back up over the cliff and down to the beach by the CLIFF café, there are danger warning signs onto the rock faces regarding falling rocks.

Baits: Some suggestions…

One:	Frozen black Lugworm pieces first then small ragworm.
Two:	Small Ragworm tipped with a small piece of Mackerel or Herring.
Three:	Blow Lugworm.
Four:	Small King Ragworm.
Five:	Crab with small Ragworm, elasticated on.
Traces:	Fixed Paternoster, Running Ledger, but you must have a long range rig for bottom water fishing Penell or pully. But at top water all change, close range rigs.

After Pendine between Dolwen Point and Gilman Point is the escape route over the cliff.

44

HISTORY AT PENDINE

"GILMAN POINT" So called because a preacher called GILMAN give a Serman at the entrance to a cave called the "PULPIT" also called "GILMAN CHURCH CAVE", and just around this section of coastline above a jumble of rocks is a rock face which resembles a human head with the nose broken off. Above which is "BEACONS HILL" where the wreckers used to place lights to ensnare unwary ships on to the rocks.

And on to a marvellous time at PENDINE the chase for the land speed records.

'Church Cave', the human head of rock, with the nose broken off!

On the 25th of September, 1925, SIR MALCOLM CAMPBELL, 146.16 m.p.h. 350 h.p. twelve cylinder Sunbeam called "BLUEBIRD". 1926, Campbell's Sunbeam "BLUEBIRD" clocked 150.81 m.p.h.

Enter the arena
J. G. PARRY-THOMAS in his car "BABS" 1926. Clocked 169.30 m.p.h. and later on in the same year came in with a speed of 171.02 m.p.h.

Still in 1926 SIR MALCOLM CAMPBELL'S Sunbeam clocked 174.88 m.p.h.

Not to be outdone J G was determined to be the first man to reach a speed of 175 m.p.h., and on March 4th 1927 made the attempt, but unfortunately met his death in the attempt. "BABS" was buried in the sand dunes and lay there from 1927 until 1969, then removed from the dunes and restored over a number of years, now at the museum at PENDINE.

45

When you walk to TWIN TOWERS just imagine driving a car at 175 MPH along this stretch of sand, it must have taken a lot of work to prepare the surface in a short period of time, but it still needed a tremendous amount of courage.

But then what happens, in 1998. DON WALES, SIR MALCOLM CAMPBELL'S grandson starts the race off again with his ELECTRIC car, setting a new British record of 116 m.p.h. Then on Sunday 17th June 2000 in "BLUEBIRD ELECTRIC" comes up with a speed of 128 m.p.h., with the electric power supplied by HAWKER GENESIS aircraft type batteries. BLUEBIRD ELECTRICS Length is 21 feet and just over four foot wide.

The world record for an electric car, (which I hope DON WALES will be chasing) is held by PAT RUMMERFIELD, an American in his car named "WHITE LIGHTNING", battery powered with banks of over 6000 batteries = speed 248 m.p.h. at BONNEVILLE SALT FLATS.

So we have: CAMPBELL *v* PARRY THOMAS
WALES *v* RUMMERFIELD
BREEDLOVE *v* ARFONS
NOBLE/GREENE *v* ????

6000 Batteries = 248 m.p.h.
100,000 Horse Power = 763 m.p.h.

'Twin Towers', Pendine.

August 5th 1963, 25 year old, CRAIG BREEDLOVE in his jet engine powered car "SPIRIT of AMERICA" with GOODYEAR tyres had the land speed record with a speed of 407.4 m.p.h.

Early October 1964, ART ARFONS in his car "GREEN MONSTER" with FIRESTONE tyres came in with a speed of 434 m.p.h.

October 15th, 1964, BREEDLOVE, 526 m.p.h. first through the 500 m.p.h. barrier.

Two weeks later ARFONS went faster.

1965, BREEDLOVE first through the 600 m.p.h. barrier, and the same year ARFONS crashed and survived at 610 MPH that was the end of Mr ART ARFONS racing.

Now comes in Mr RICHARD NOBLE. October 4th 1983 in "THRUST 2" with ALUMINUM wheels at BLACK ROCK NEVADA DESERT. 633 m.p.h.

September 1997, Mr ANDY GREENE, a jet pilot took over the wheel of RICHARD NOBLES car "THRUST SSC", 54 foot long, and 100,000 Horse Power! set a speed of 763.035 m.p.h.

Now back to PENDINE M.O.D. RANGE, wind tests were carried out for THRUST SSC, I tried to find out some more information, but none were forthcoming.

Between Ginst and Pendine, with Worms Head in the background.

47

Morfa-Bychan (Little boy) or Pebble Beach

Camping/Caravans	No
Disabled	No
Bait	No
Seafood	No

Directions

Coming over the Bridge, Cardiff or the Valley's take the M4 Motorway to CARMARTHEN, straight on at the first roundabout, left at the second A40 to ST. CLEARS. Turn left after travelling under the third road bridge A4066 signposted LAUGHARNE/PENDINE, drive through LAUGHARNE, BROADWAY-BROOK, LLANMILOE, through PENDINE up the hill and take the left hand road towards AMROTH. After you pass the "GREENBRIDGE" public house (if it is still open after publishing) take the next lane left with the damaged walking sign alongside.

Between one and two miles to MORFA BYCHAN BAY.

Morfa-Bychan beach.

Venue 1: "Brinkspier" Look-Out Post (NGR 22.6/07.5)

Drive down slowly the narrow rough lane for just over one mile to the bay, difficult passing manoeuvres. So lets have a walk to the bay down through MORFA BYCHAN valley towards dusk *(to fish for small TOPE on the left hand side)* eerie with legends and mysteries, is it a ruined farm cottage in amongst the trees on the right hand side?

I fished this venue twice during the twilight hours before you were able to take the car down (iron rods etc. poking up out of the unmade road – strange).

The ugly pumping station.

There is a subterranean water passage in the valley of the "GREENBRIDGE of WALES" with the water board in 1984 made some improvements to the water passage down the valley, then calling it the PENDINE STREAM. But what about improving the appearance of the UGLY PUMPING STATION on the right hand side!.

Arriving at the bay you come to a high bank of shingle, and in the middle of the beach "BRINKSPIER" shelter, the remains of a world war two wall, behind which is the only shelter on a wild and windswept bay. Sand to steep stone/shingle with cliffs on both sides. No need to cast long distances on a high tide towards top water.

No bait available other than searching out some crab on the right hand side, problem is there is a lot of fresh water rushing out to the sea.

Fish BRINKSPIER wall and working over to the left hand side.

Species and traces as PENDINE, add a lightweight TOPE trace.

Marros and Telpyn Point

Camping/Caravans	Members Only
Disabled	No
Bait	Very limited
Seafood	Laver Weed, Winkles

Directions

Coming over the SEVERN bridge or down from the VALLEY'S to CARMARTHEN. Straight on at the first roundabout, left at the second A40 to ST. CLEARS, turn left after travelling under the third road bridge A4066 LAUGHARNE-PENDINE.

Drive through LAUGHARNE, BROADWAY-BROOK, LLANMILOE, through PENDINE up the steep hill to the AMROTH road sign, two miles to go to "SAINT LAWRENCE CHURCH" at MARROS, to park on the grass verge by the telephone box, the lane by the church is private property, with no parking signs.

Walk down the lane past three farms, then after "PLEASANT VIEW" bungalow its straight on through a gate in front of you, or by means of a gap on the left hand side. If someone has left the gate open – please close.

You can now see "WORMS HEAD" on the GOWER PENINSULA in the distance, now starts the steep hill down to MARROS beach, turn left at the sign UNDERHILL.

Marros beach and the wreck of the 'Rover'.

MARROS and TELPYN, because of their locality only the more rugged and "Sun Worshipers" (*Skinny Dippers!*) use the beach. Therefore, especially if there has been a nice blow out to sea three or four tides previous, and a nice surf running to test your skills as a BASS fisherman/woman. Relatively flat sandy beach interspaced with peat beds. And shingle at top water.

Bait: At bottom water after a high tide, very limited amount of RAZOR FISH, and scattered VENUS SHELL CLAMS, the best chance of obtaining BLOW LUGWORM is just before the rocks towards TELPYN POINT, and amongst the stones for crab during the warmer months, but its not a piece of cake to obtain any of the above baits.

Laver Weed in season on the stones in front of "UNDERHILL HOUSE".

So now to the fishing.

The waterfall at
Telpyn Point.

Venue 1: Top Castle (NGR 19.4/07.4)

Towards TELPYN before the rocks with a single cave at your back and the waterfall on the right. I enjoy this venue in front of the cliffs, where the flat stone look as if they have been placed on top of each other up and over the caves. Some care required at this venue as the tide is making, so move over to the left casting as you go until you come to a gap in the peat beds, and the sand is rippled where salt and freshwater meet.

Venue 2: Rover Point (NGR 21.7/07.1)

From one extreme end of the beach to the other. You are now walking towards RAGWEN POINT with a buoy out in the bay, walk along the beach towards the top water mark, and in the sand you will come to the wreck of the "COAL KETCH", a two masted sailing vessel the "ROVER" with her oak ribs sticking up out of the sand, stranded in 1873. Carry on past this point for a further 300-400 yards to fish where the rock and peat beds are further down the sandy beach, it's a good walk from the entrance to the beach.

Venue 3: Freshwater Stream (NGR 20.3/07.4)

In front of UNDERHILL HOUSE, start over to the left hand side, and after every cast move to the right about ten yards. The seagulls seem to like this area!

Venue 4: Bridge Point Bay (NGR 18.3/07.2).

Now to conclude this section of coastline, we move on to TELYN POINT. Walk back to the car, coming down about one and three quarters of a mile a long hard steep slog, seems at least double going back.

Drive towards AMROTH for two miles to a small lay by with a walking sign alongside, just after TELPYN farm with its clay pigeon shooting *(telephone number PENDINE 633)*. Now a shorter walk down a muddy lane through the woods to *venue 4*. Because of the make up of this section of sand, and distribution of rock and peat, there seems to be a lot more movement of water at top tide. Worth a try for Mackerel in the Summer off the rocks.

Both areas remote – so take a mobile phone.

TELPYN POINT is the end of the Carmarthenshire Coastal Path.

Amroth

Camping/Caravans	Yes and self catering at the Castle, Telephone Number: 01834 813217
Disabled	Difficult at top water
Bait	Very limited. Black & Blow Lugworm Razorfish, Crab, & Venus Shells
Seafood	Laver Weed, and try some fresh Razorfish

Directions

Arriving at CARMARTHEN, straight on at the first roundabout, left at the second A40 ST. CLEARS turn left after travelling under the third road bridge A4066 LAUGHARNE/PENDINE. Drive through LAUGHARNE, BROADWAY-BROOK, LLANMILOE, through PENDINE up the steep hill, turn left at the top signposted AMROTH. just past here is GROVE holiday park tourer caravan site (NGR 22.4/07.5) telephone number: 01994 453469, on past TELPYN FARM, CLAY PIGEON SHOOTING (NGR 18.6/07.5) telephone number: PENDINE 633. And so on to the NEW INN PUBLIC HOUSE, the start of the 186 Mile long PEMBROKESHIRE COASTAL PATH. Opened on the 16th MAY, 1970, by WYNFORD VAUGHAN THOMAS.

Amroth

Amroth is a flat sandy beach with a high bank of pebbles at top water. With 23 Wooden Sea Defence Groynes running down to the sea. I have numbered them from *Number 1* Which is in front of the "TEMPLE BAR INN".

Bait: Very scarce. Razor Fish and some Lugworm at bottom water in front of the castle, more chance of obtaining on a really big tide, Crab and Black Lugworm near "BLACKSMITH SHOP" *Venue 1.*
  You must bring bait with you, but for the Winter competitions you must have Blast Frozen Sand Eels with the head and tail removed, Clipped down casting into the "GULLY" a long way out in front of the "NEW INN" public house. Elasticate the small eels on.

Species – Winter: Poor Whiting, and small Flounder. Dogfish far out either end of the bay.

Species – Summer: Bass, and Flounder with the very occasional Mullet, try some long cast spinning for Mackerel at top water. But mainly a bottom water fishing beach.

Rigs: Running Ledger-Paternoster-Clipped, Snood, Paternoster-Pully-Penell.

Venue 1: "Blacksmith Shop" (NGR 15.3/06.3)

It is the area known locally towards WISEMANS BRIDGE past the caves, a rocky area with high cliffs at your back. Care required when the tide is making, and a fair distance to walk with all your tackle from the small car park in front of the "TEMPLE BAR INN".

Venue 2: "Amroth Arms" (NGR 16.4/06.1)

Either side of the stream, between *Groyne Number 1 and 4.* Parking near the public house.

Venue 3: "Fir Tree" (NGR 17.O/07.0)

Between the fir tree and the slipway, the stream comes out near groyne *Number 9.* Park near the AMROTH ARMS, walk up the hill and down onto the beach near the post office, you can see the single fir tree at your back near this point, or you can drive the car further along the foreshore and park in front of the castle entrance, cross the road and walk down the slipway to the beach.

Venue 4: "New Inn" (NGR 17.4/07.0)

The NEW INN Public house is after *Groyne Number 23,* the river emerges from under the pebbles onto the beach, after starting it's journey at TAVERNSPITE and running down through CLYN-GWYNNE VALLEY.

Start fishing one hour before bottom water, casting as far as possible in to a so called "GULLY", This is one of the venues that distance counts, then as the tide makes you will have passed a peat bed on the way down to fish, some 50 yards long with the remains of a couple of tree stumps, try casting on to this peat bed as long as possible.

LAVER WEED *(LAVERBREAD)* Small amounts in front of the post office, attached to the large jumble of rocks seaward side, it's the small black weed stuck flat to the rocks, and some weed attached to the rocks between the low number groynes.

Footnote: About three miles from AMROTH at LUDCHURCH, Lieutenant Commander MARTIN Lies buried. He was the last officer to have accompanied Captain Cook on his expeditions to Australia. On his grave are the words, He made Seven Voyages around the world.

Wisemans Bridge

Camping/Caravans	Meadowhouse and Oakland, also book in at the Wisemans Bridge public house
Disabled	No
Bait	No
Seafood	No

Directions

CARMARTHEN, straight on at the first roundabout, left at the second A40. Follow this road until you come to the large ST. CLEARS roundabout, take the road to PEMBROKE A477, drive through RED ROSES, LLANTEG, then watch for the sign AMROTH 2¼ miles, LUDCHURCH 2½ miles, WISEMANS BRIDGE 2½ miles. Well sign posted. Drive straight through SUMMERHILL, the sign to WISEMANS BRIDGE at this point is a little bit obscure, but do not turn left down to AMROTH, but drive down the hill passing MEADOW HOUSE and OAKLAND caravan parks, to park by the WISEMANS BRIDGE Public House.

The Storm Beach Hamlet of WISEMANS BRIDGE is a mixture of clean sand-rocks, and large pebbles at the top water mark.

Wisemans Bridge

Venue 1: Churchill and Monty Rocks (NGR 15.1/06.1)

To the left of the pub for about 600 yards to a small sandy inlet adjoined by flat black rocks, covered in small Mussel, and the so called *Coal Measure Cliffs* at your back. Further over to your left, the rocks of the "BLACKSMITH SHOP".

Bait: Always popular are the small Harbour Ragworm, but a mixture of Black Lugworm – Blow Lugworm, and Fish baits are worth a try. Elasticate Crab and Mussel on together.

Rigs: Bottom water, tune your reel for distance casting, with a pully type rig, as it is quite a steep beach adjust the reel for closer casts towards top water.

Venue 2: Fossil Bay (NGR 14.5/05.8)

Drive towards the Tunnels and COPPIT HALL across the small "PLEASANT VALLEY" Trout Stream, not a lot of room to park near the phone box, more room before the trout stream. Walk towards the Tunnels to fish the lovely sandy bay, access is just after the safety hand railing and warning sign. Whilst fishing this venue towards the latter part of 2001, the *Fossil Hunters* were chipping away at the rocks at my back?

Small Flounder and the occasional Bass. Bring bait with you to help what you can find, to alternate with fish and sandeel.

Footnote: Whilst walking along the STRAND towards the Tunnels. The cliff faces are now braced off with wire mesh, and the Iron Ore Mine Levels are closed off with Stainless Steel Bars, but imagine a small Steam Train transporting coal along the narrow gauge railway track. Rumour has it that the local authority are considering re-opening this track. Is it possible? I would love to see some sort of track through the tunnels along the coastline, but I doubt it, what a pity.

The name of the little steam train was the "ROSALIND or ROSSLYN", driven by amongst others Mr JOHN BRINN.

Rehearsals were carried out at WISEMANS during the 1939-45 War for the D Day Landing with CHURCHILL, MONTGOMERY, EISENHOWER in attendance.

Coppit Hall

Camping/Caravans	No
Disabled	No
Bait	No
Seafood	Winkles, poor Mussel

Directions

From CARMARTHEN take the A40 to the large ST. CLEARS round-about, then take the A477 towards PEMBROKE, through RED ROSES and LLANTEG, then watch for the sign to AMROTH, LUDCHURCH, WISEMANS BRIDGE 2 miles, well signposted to WISEMANS BRIDGE *(Do not take the road down to Amroth).*

Drive along the narrow road past the WISEMANS BRIDGE INN over PLEASANT VALLEY Trout Stream, up the hill and follow the road until you come to COPPIT HALL car park on the left hand side. Car parking charge during the summer months. Free Winter.

A short journey from here to SAUNDERSFOOT.

The tunnel from Wisemans Bridge and Coppit Hall beach.

The steep shelving bay interspaced with rocks in the middle. The beach is only about 600 Yards in width before it joins up with SAUNDERSFOOT BAY.

Venue 1: (NGR 14.1/05.3)

Over to the left hand side of the bay, fishing amongst the mixture of sand and flat sloping rocks.

Start fishing at bottom water during the latter part of the year with clipped down rigs baited with blast frozen Sand Eel with the head and tail removed, and tied on with thin elasticated cotton. Dogfish way out in the bay.

I am not a lover of frozen Sand Eel, but here is a beach where they are worth a try, also try using a bunch of small Ragworm tipped and tied off with a small piece of Razor Fish.

Summer Months: Fish in the rain, or on a nice day go further over to the left and search out a small gully amongst the rocks. Fish with a rotten bottom rig, or try a small bubble float with Peeler or Soft Crab on a Treble or Double Hook.

Coppit Hall beach.

Saundersfoot

Camping/Caravans	Yes
Disabled	Parking: As you come down the hill turn left opposite the Royal Oak public house to park along the Strand
Bait	Very limited, Razor Fish, Lugworm, Cockles, poor Crab
Seafood	Cockles, Laverweed, Winkles, poor Mussel

Directions

From the CARDIFF and SEVERN BRIDGE areas, come down the M4 Motorway to the first Roundabout at CARMARTHEN *(It is 9 Miles to the ST. CLEARS Roundabout from here)*, straight on at this roundabout, left at the next A40 all the way to the ST. CLEARS roundabout, then take the A478 TENBY Road through LLANDDOWROR, RED ROSES, LLANTEG. Arriving at the KILGETTY roundabout, *(21 Miles from the first roundabout at Carmarthen)* take the B4316 Saundesfoot road, up the hill turn left, Saundesfoot B4316, Opposite HILL PARK Caravan Park, Driving down into Saundersfoot.

Saundersfoot Harbour.

This section of coastline is extremely busy during the Summer Months, no way will you be able to fish the beach to the left of the harbour. Therefore, try the following.

Top Water, off the Harbour Wall, only accessible on the walkway on the right of the harbour past the yacht club, very popular but I prefer to fish the Coves to the right hand side towards TENBY 3³/₄ miles distant.

The Coves: HARBOUR, GLEN, PERRIS, SMALLTREE, RHODE WOOD, JOHNY'S. All before MONKSTONE POINT, but beware the tide will cut you off along this stretch especially on a high tide, so make sure you have a escape route, they are there. I like fishing near the KILN STEPS (NGR 14.0/03.9) leading up to the RHODE WOODS and the Caravan Park.

Razor Fish used to be plentiful, but now dug out so a lesson should be learned to preserve what we have in relation to all sorts of baits. Bring bait with you for Bass, Flounder and troublesome Dogfish latter part of the year.

Access for a wheelchair is a ramp down to the beach on the right hand side of the Harbour. Booking in for boat trips, and a small tackle shop for bits and pieces on the right hand side, both for me a little bit expensive.

Car Parking Charges range from £1.50 to £2.50, but each year increasing, but you can get to the COVES by driving up the hill out of SAUNDERSFOOT towards TENBY, and after passing the ST. BRIDES HOTEL take the first left down GLEN ROAD to park at the bottom by the no tipping sign. One way to the beach is alongside a small waterfall, or up through the woods and down the wooden slatted steps to emerge by the "LADY CAVE ANTICLINE" nice cave to shelter out of the wind and rain.

Footnote: In 1764 there were 2 houses in SAUNDERSFOOT (Where were they built?). I am told there were 30 in 1945. How many now? The Harbour was built between 1829 and 1835 at a cost of £7000.

Monkstone Point

Camping/Caravans	Trevayne Farm
Disabled	No
Bait	No
Seafood	No

Directions

At the first roundabout at CARMARTHEN *(You have 23.8 MILES from here to the NEW HEDGES roundabout)* straight on, left at the second A40 to the large ST. CLEARS roundabout, which is some 9 Miles distant, then take the A478 TENBY ROAD through LLANDD-OWROR, RED ROSES, LLANTEG, up to the KILGETTY roundabout, take the A478 TENBY road driving through WOODEN CRANE CROSS to the NEW HEDGES roundabout. Turn left, B4316, then SHARP RIGHT at the sign to TREVAYNE FARM which is on a square stone block, drive down the lane and park near the farm – check regarding payment, but please do not cause an obstruction the Farmer kindly allows us access to the beautiful bay.

Monkstone Point.

The cliffs at your back, Monkstone Point.

If you decide to walk from SAUNDERSFOOT to fish this venue it is approximately one and a half miles when the tide is out, then clambering over the rocks to reach MONKSTONE POINT.

From TREVAYNE FARM the way to the beach is on a wooden signpost. *NB: Travel light because the way down is very-very steep down wooden slatted steps, slippery when the leaves are falling.*

When you eventually get to the beach it is well worth the effort peaceful and beautiful sands, pebbles at top water for 20 Yards then on to very clean sand.

Venue 1: Grail Rock (NGR 14.8/03.2)

Walk over to the left casting into a sandy gully as the tide makes between the rocks. Take some fish bait down with you, to try for some Dabs. Difficult escape route up over the cliff face.

Some 17 to 20 miles distant is LLANMADOC HILL and RHOSSILI DOWN on the GOWER PENINSULA.

Waterwynch

Camping/Caravans	No
Disabled	No
Bait	No
Seafood	No

Directions

From the Severn Bridge come down the M4 Motorway to the first roundabout at Carmarthen *(25 Miles to go to TENBY)*, straight on at this roundabout, left at the second A40 to ST. CLEARS roundabout, then go on to the A478 TENBY road through LLANDDOWROR, RED ROSES, LLANTEG, up to the KILGETTY roundabout. Carry on the A478 TENBY road through WOODEN CRANE CROSS, up to the New Hedges roundabout, follow the TENBY sign A478 then watch for the sign "ROWSTON" Holiday Park because just after this on the left is the sign for WATERWYNCH HUNTING LODGE and DINGLE COTTAGE, you will have to park at the top of the lane. Private Road.

Waterwynch Bay.

After parking, walk down the private road towards the Hunting Lodge until you come to the Beach sign, following the leaf strewn lane and then down the sunken path steps to the beach. Some $\frac{1}{2}$ mile down, seems like a mile back up to the car.

High bank of pebbles towards top water. Very difficult unproductive venue coping with the sea weed and rubbish being washed up between the narrow rock faced cove, on the incoming tide and the rushing freshwater stream tumbling seawards.

Venue 1: (NGR 13.8/02.0)

Fish between the Cliffs. One Hour out from bottom water, and perhaps two hours on the incoming, depending on conditions.

Bait: Try Lugworm, Blow and Black, tipped with a strip of Squid. Or Ragworm tipped with a small strip of fish baits, to help retaining the bait during casting.

Traces: Pully, Pennell, Running Paternoster.

Spiny Spider Crab.

Tenby

Camping/Caravans	Yes
Disabled	Yes. Harbour Wall, Pennyless Cove, Gosker Wall
Bait	Very limited
Seafood	Laver Weed

Directions

Arriving at the first roundabout at CARMARTHEN *(25 miles to Tenby)* straight on, left at the second A40 to the ST. CLEARS roundabout, then on to the A478 TENBY road, through LLANDDOWROR, RED ROSES, LLANTEG to the KILGETTY roundabout, take the A478 TENBY road through WOODEN-CRANE CROSS up to the NEW HEDGES roundabout straight on, and when entering TENBY follow the NORTH BEACH sign driving through the town to park. (Parking is difficult Summer Months)

DISABLED PARKING: Three Positions near the Coast Guard Hut, and a number at the bottom of "PENNYLESS COVE HILL". Just to the left of the hut, at the top of the hill down to the harbour.

Gosker Rock, Tenby.

Venue 1: Gosker Rock – Bowmans Point (NGR 13.2/00.7)

Walk down PENNYLESS COVE HILL *(Just before the Coast Guard Hut).* To fish along this stretch of bay from the start of North Beach in front of Gosker Rock, and out to Bowman's Point.

Bait: Laver Weed & poor Mussel on Table Rock, near Bowman's Point.

Venue 2: Harbour Wall (NGR 13.8/00.7)

Walk down the hill to the harbour, to fish near the end into the main channel. Summer Months try for MULLET. *(See Mullet Paste)*
There are a couple of old CANNON'S used as Bollards on the Harbour!

Venue 3: Iron Bar Beach (NGR 13.6/00.3)

At the top of the Harbour hill turn right down the Slipway past the toilets to fish IRON BAR BEACH in front of ST. CATHERINES ISLAND.

Species: Bass. Must be on a wet and windy day in the Summer. Species caught around TENBY:- Bass, Flounder, Mullet, Ballen Wrasse, Some Conger and Trigger Fish South Beach under GILTER POINT.

Footnote: On the Seaward side of ST. CATHERINES is SKER ROCK and further out to sea WOOLHOUSE ROCK, not always visible, on top of which before the days of Lifeboats was a high pole with a cage on top, to enable up to 14 Shipwrecked Sailors to clamber up, now collapsed below water. A popular Diving area.
The first Lighthouse was positioned at CALDY ISLAND in 1829
Couple of TENBY'S famous, AUGUSTUS JOHN the Artist, ROBERT RECORDE Mathematician who invented the equals (=) sign, and brought Algebra to Britain.
TENBY has it's own DAFFODIL, found nowhere else, Gold/ Yellow, and almost a Foot Tall with a distinctive trumpet. With a marvellous name of NARCISSUS OBVALLARIS.
I would like to thank Mrs Sue Baldwin of TENBY MUSEUM for information about the area.

Gilter

Camping/Caravans	No
Disabled	No
Bait	No
Seafood	No

Directions

Arriving at the first roundabout at CARMARTHEN from the Valley's, straight on at the first, left at the second roundabout A40 to the large ST. CLEARS roundabout, then on to the A478 TENBY road, through LLANDDOWROR, RED ROSES, LLANTEG to the KILGETTY roundabout, follow the A478 TENBY road through WOODEN-CRANE CROSS up to the NEW HEDGES roundabout, follow the road into TENBY, driving down the hill through two small roundabouts and out of the town on the Pembroke road A4139 passing KILN PARK on your left, then watch for the PENALLY Railway Station car park.

Cross over the railway track and walk out over the PENALLY Camp M.O.D marshlands, passing over the TENBY Golf Course, just under half a mile to the beach.

Gilter Head, 'Sewer Pipe Cove'.

Venue 1: Burrows Sand Bar (NGR 12.4/99.5)

Arriving at the beach go over to the left almost mid way to IRON BAR BEACH, there is a sand bar along this stretch with gullies, along which the Bass patrol searching out food. Long casts with clipped down rigs, start from bottom water on the flood.

Venue 2: Sewer Pipe Cove (NGR 12.3/98.4)

Turn right at the beach towards GILTER POINT to fish the other side of the disused/collapsed sewer pipe on the small bay below the cliffs. If MAY WEED or SEA WEED is troublesome go back over the outfall pipe to fish the so called "WHITE SANDS" where it appears that for some reason the water temperature is very slightly higher! On a very high spring tide there is evidence of a Medieval Fish Trap System, approximately 250 Paces towards the TENBY End, after the ramp hidden amongst the stones.

Try fishing this venue at bottom water, to catch the first run of the tide, beneath Gilter Head.

Venue 3: Gilter Head (NGR 12.5/98.4)

Take the Cliff path up over GILTER and watch for the path on the left to take you down to the rocks to fish the incoming tide.

Species: WRASSE, STRAP CONGER, BASS with CRAB, WHITING, DAB, DOGFISH. Chance of a RAY with Fish Baits. Lots of choices.

Rigs – Summer Months: Try with a Plug or Spinner, or on a very warm still day practice your Fly Fishing skills with a Bass Fly.

GILTER HEAD – If you are a little bit crazy and fleet of foot, as some of the locals are, fish down off "HIDDEN SLABS" on GILTER HEAD into deep water for a variety of species, with CALDY and ST. MARGARET'S ISLAND facing you. So be warned DANGER.

Lots of beautiful areas to explore, just to name a few. DAWN BAY, BECKS BAY, PROUD GILTER, FUNNEL HOLE, and on to LYDSTEP.

I would like to thank Mr George Cavill of PENALLY *(with whom I spent a very pleasant hour or so out on GILTER)* for information about the area.

Lydstep

Camping/Caravans	Yes
Disabled	No
Bait	No
Seafood	No

Directions

At CARMARTHEN, follow the A40 to the big ST. CLEARS roundabout some 8 miles distant, then on to the A478 TENBY road, through LLANDDOWROR, RED ROSES, LLANTEG. Left at the KILGETTY roundabout A478 TENBY road through WOODEN-CRANE CROSS up to the NEW HEDGES roundabout on into TENBY, down the hill through two small roundabouts and out of the town on the PEMBROKE road A4139 passing PENALLY railway station and LYDSTEP holiday park *(private site)*. Drive into LYDSTEP village, and after passing the LYSTEP TAVERN public house turn left at the dead end sign, down an unmade road to park just before the exit of LYDSTEP holiday park near a small boat yard. No obstructions please.

Way down to Lydstep Bay.

Lydstep buttress rocks.

Venue 1: Lydstep Pinnacle (NGR 09.3/97.8)

After parking, walk down and turn right out towards the rocks to fish close to the PINNACLES. Winter venue as the holiday village is so popular and the bay is always busy.

Venue 2: Lydstep Caverns (NGR 09.3/97.5)

Before you go all the way down the lane *(see directions)* drive up the leaf covered lane opposite BOWLAND Caravan Park, over the wide roll bar cattle grid. Beware at this time there are deep potholes to dodge before parking.

On LYDSTEP HEAD follow the ACORN Symbol signposts until you come to the way down the one 'hundred and eleven' very unequal man made steps.

Opposite you can see the pathways from "BETSY BRINN'S" Cottage, unfortunately now long demolished.

This is a extremely difficult venue with high tackle losses between the Slab Buttress Rocks. Rotten bottom rigs. Only able to fish this venue at bottom water.

But if you like exploring, and travelling light with a fishing rod. Try this difficult stretch of coastline with just nesting sea birds for company, making your way over to WHITE TOWER, BRAZEN BUTTRESS, MOTHER CAREY'S KITCHEN. Passing WHITE SHEET ROCK on to LYDSTEP CAVERN BAY, SKOMER BAY, SKOMER TOWERS and on to SKRINKLE.

Skrinkle Haven & Presipe Bay

Camping/Caravans	No
Disabled	No
Bait	No
Seafood	No

Directions

A40 out of CARMARTHEN, then at the big ST. CLEARS roundabout take the A478 TENBY road to the KILGETTY roundabout. Follow the A478 to TENBY, down the hill passing through two small roundabouts and out of the town on the A4139 PEMBROKE road, passing PENALLY Railway Station, through LYDSTEP then take the MANORBIER, SKRINKLE HAVEN road B4585, turning left at the sign SKRINKLE HAVEN YOUTH HOSTEL, drive up towards the Ministry of Defence gate turning left before the entrance, to drive down to the YOUTH HOSTEL car park.

Skrinkle Haven.

Presipe Bay.

Venue 1: Church Doors (NGR 08.3/97.4)

Park in the Youth Hostel car park and follow the coast path sign down the steep access steps *(NB: Heed the warning sign at the top of the steps regarding SKINKLE HAVEN being a cut off venue).*

Bottom water venue only. Pebbles then clean sand, the Church Doors are on you left (features in the rock face).

Beautiful area of coastline, worth a walk along the headland both ways, but if you are afraid of heights this area is not for the faint hearted. So a little care required.

Venue 2: Presipe Bay (NGR 07.2/ 96.9)

Driving up to the M. O. D. entrance, park on the road just before the gate, then go over the stile on the right hand side, and keeping to the fence follow the Pembrokeshire Coastal Acorn signs for about one mile over the windy downs and down 95 Steps to PRESIPE BAY.

Lovely sandy bay and coves at bottom water. Try this venue as soon as the sand becomes exposed.

Manorbier

Camping/Caravans	Surrounding areas
Disabled	Yes, with some help
Bait	No
Seafood	No

Directions

From the Severn Bridge and the surrounding areas, when you arrive at the first roundabout at CARMARTHEN *(You have 31.2 miles to go to MANORBIER)* straight on at the first, left at the second A40, eight Miles to the ST. CLEARS roundabout onto the A478 TENBY road, through LLANDDOWROR, RED ROSES, LLANTEG to the KILGETTY roundabout, carry straight on through TENBY down the hill through two small roundabouts and out of the town on the PEMBROKE road A4139 passing KILN PARK Holiday Park. PENNALY Railway Station, through LYDSTEP then take the MANORBIER B4585 road driving down through MANORBIER Village to the beach car park – signposted.

Manorbier Castle. You can just see the access bridge for disabled fishing.

74

Venue 1: Blue Badge (NGR 06.1/97.5)

Difficult but with some assistance, from the car park along the path and over a small footbridge to fish to the right near a small waterfall. Top water on a high tide.

Venue 2: Main Beach (NGR 06.1/97.4)

Too busy Summer Months, so try later on in the year – night time, or inclement weather.

Venue 3: Dak Cove (NGR 05.8/97.6)

To the right of the of the beach off the rocks towards "DAKS" Cove.

Rigs: Feathers, Plugs, Spinning. Have you thought of Fly Fishing on a warm still day, give it a try with the modern "BASS FLIES".

Venue 4: Priest's Nose (NGR 05.9/97.2)

Walk to the left of the beach up the steps and out along the cliff path, passing the "KINGS QUOIT" Burial Chamber *(How many men and women managed to lift the huge Capstone with home made ropes and pulley's into position?)* to descend down the Priests Nose to fish into deep water *(NB: There is danger here)*. Nearly $^3/_4$ of a mile from the car park.

A lovely fresh water stream comes down from the Castle, winding it's way out onto the beach over the shingle and out into the bay over clean sand.

I'm informed but cannot substantiate the species caught at this venue. Conger by night, Pollack and Wrasse by day, Mackerel and Garfish, but unfortunately no information regarding our Bass.

In front of you over the wall at the car park is a sandy scrubland, to the left of the ruined mill GIRALDUS, born at MANORBIER in 1146, had his Orchards and Vineyards around about 1166. Were they fed by the beautiful clean stream, probably not.

What a lovely name for a truly Welsh wine: GILALDUS RED! GILALDUS WHITE!

Swanlake Bay

Camping/Caravans	Yes
Disabled	No
Bait	No
Seafood	No

Directions

CARMATHEN to TENBY. Then from PENALLY Railway Station, driving through LYDSTEP village, then taking the MANORBIER road B4585 down and out of MANORBIER, up the hill for just over one and a half miles to a small crossroads, turn left and watch for the sign "EASTMOOR FARM" and SWANLAKE BAY camping, drive up the potholed road to park near the farm.

Please do not cause an obstruction, farm machinery in constant use.

Swanlake Bay.

Swanlake Bay from East Moor Farm.

Venue 1: Swanlake Bay (NGR 04.6/97.8)

The Farm area and path are muddy during the Winter months. Walk across in front of East Moor Farm House, and follow the coastal path over a couple of fields *(Be careful when approaching the round cattle water/feeding station, deep sticky mud)* for just about half a mile to the sandy bay down past some stone cottage ruins, search out the more stony areas of the bay.

Baits: Experiment with baits. Sandeel head and tail removed. Frozen Crab. Lugworm tipped with Razor Fish. Harbour Ragworm.

Rigs: Long casts with clipped down rigs. Pennel, Pulley Double Patting, and if you can manage it take two rods down to the bay.

Freshwater East

Camping/Caravans	Yes
Disabled	No
Bait	No
Seafood	No

Directions

From the Cardiff, Newport and the Severn Bridge areas drive down to CARMARTHEN, straight on at the first roundabout *(37 miles to go to FRESHWATER EAST)* at the second roundabout turn left A40 ST. CLEARS, and after some 8 miles take the A478 TENBY road, drive through TENBY down the hill through two small roundabouts and out of the town on the PEMBROKE road A4139, stay on this road through PENALLY, LYDSTEP, JAMESTON and HODGESTON, then follow the sign FRESHWATER EAST B4584. Turning right at the sign to the beach TREWENT and STACKPOLE, to park at the beach car parks.

Disabled parking only nearest to the beach.

Freshwater East Bay.

Venue 1: Trewent Point (NGR 01.9/97.4)

A freshwater stream runs out into the bay over shingle to a large clean sandy beach. Cross over the wooden footbridge to fish to the right of the beach near the rocks towards TREWENT POINT.

Bait: Search out the odd crab or two amongst the rocks in season.

3 Miles to STACKPOLE.

Stackpole

Camping/Caravans	No
Disabled	No
Bait	No
Seafood	No

Directions

From the FRESWATER EAST car park, go up the hill, STACKPOLE road, passing FRESHWATER Bay holiday village, driving through EAST TREWENT. Follow the sign to STACKPOLE, turning left at the dead end sign STACKPOLE QUAY/BARAFUNDLE, to park at the beach car park.

39 miles from the first roundabout at CARMARTHEN.

Stackpole Quay. The smallest harbour in Britain.

Venue 1: Stackpole Wall (NGR 99.3/ 95.7)

Britains smallest harbour.

After parking walk down the lane to the rocky foreshore of the quay.

If you do decide to fish off the wall and the tide cuts you off, there is an escape route ladder at the small sandy cove up and over the cliff face.

Bottom water fish at the entrance of the small harbour mouth casting slightly to the left to miss the marker buoys.

Top water fish off the wall on the extreme left hand side, casting straight out into the bay

See my distance rotten bottom rig.

Rigs: All rigs should be clipped down, because the sea area in front of you looks awesome, but be brave and give it a long range cast. The fish are there.

Barafundle

Camping/Caravans	No
Disabled	No
Bait	No
Seafood	No

Directions

From the STACKPOLE car park, the path to BARAFUNDLE is signposted up 48 wooden slatted steps and out over the headland to a absolutely beautiful sandy bay, to descend through the archway to the beach. Voted in 2004 the best beach in WALES.

Looking at the wall above the bay, it was built by the Bricklayers working for the CAWDOR family some 200 Years ago, still in good order.

Approximately one mile from the car park.

Barafundle Bay lattice windows.

Venue 1: Barafundle Bay (NGR 99.2 / 94.9)

Walk over to the right hand side of the beach close to the rocks.

Lively surf beach after a blow out to sea, so cast out over the surf for the occasional Bass. A variety of species can be caught off the rocks. Try for Mackerel with feathers, spinning, plugs.

Because the beach is so popular you will have to search out a venue out towards the headland.

As you descend down to the bay looking over to the rocks. You are looking at GRIFFITH LORTS HOLE, a lattice type hole in the rocks.

Bosherton Lily Pond.

Broad Haven

Camping/Caravans	No
Disabled	No
Bait	No
Seafood	No

Directions

Arriving at the first roundabout at CARMARTHEN from SWANSEA and the surrounding areas, straight on, left at the second A40 to ST. CLEARS roundabout *(some 8 miles distant)* then on to the A478 down and out of TENBY on the PEMBROKE road A4139, staying on this road through LYDSTEP, JAMESTON, HODESTON and LAMPHEY, then watch for the sign FRESHWATER EAST A4584. Continue on into BOSHERTON to park at the Lily Pond car park.

If you are coming from the FRESHWATER EAST area come up STACKPOLE Road, passing FRESHWATER Bay Holiday Village, driving through EAST TREWENT. Continue straight on at the cross roads, through STACKPOLE village passing the STACKPOLE INN on your right, along the forest road up to the 'T' junction, then turn left to BOSHERTON to the lily pond car park.

Permits for Coarse Fishing at the YE OLDE WORLDE Café
Telephone Number: BOSHERTON 01646 661216.

There are three ways to reach BROAD HAVEN, two scenic and one down off the Headland.

Route 1: From Lilly Pond car park go down the steps, then take the right hand path past the small red brick building, following the muddy path out to the sandy beach. Coarse Fishing Pegs marked along this stretch, Permits to fish required.

Route 2: Again go down the steps, but now take the left hand path to cross the pond on a causeway type bridge, follow the narrow path across another small bridge, up the hill turning right signposted MIDDLE ARM, then down crossing 'GREEN BRIDGE' or 'GRASSY BRIDGE' and out to the beach.

Route 3: Drive further up to the village, turning left at the sign BROAD HAVEN, down the narrow road to park at the Headland car park, then down to the beach.

Venue 1: Saddle Point (NGR 98.0 / 94.0)

'Star Rock', Broad Haven Bay.

Venue 2: Star Rock (NGR 97.8 / 93.8)

A good Storm Beach for Bass and Flounder to Worm Baits. Tipped with Black Lugworm, or a thin slice of Mackerel or Squid to help retain the bait whilst casting.

Possibly the last Beach to fish for BASS in PEMBROKESHIRE up to the middle of October.

Difficult fishing during the Summer Months, the bay is so popular search out a quiet mark.

This is all you should leave on the beach!

St. Govans Head

Camping/Caravans	No
Disabled	No
Bait	Poor Mussel
Seafood	Small amount of Laver Weed

Directions

At the second roundabout at CARMARTHEN, take the A40 to the ST. CLEARS roundabout, then on to the A478 TENBY road, down and out of TENBY on the PEMBROKE road A4139, through LYDSTEP, JAMESTON, HODESTON and LAMPHEY. Then watch for the sign FRESHWATER EAST A4584, follow the signs for FRESHWATER EAST BEACH, EAST TREWENT, STACKPOLE and to BOSHERTON. Passing ST. GOVANS INN, BUCKS POOL FARM, The ROYAL NAVY CONTROL TOWER, and on to the car park and picnic area.

If you fancy a walk Westwards for some stunning views over NEWTON HEAD, STENNIS FORD and HUNTSMAN LEAP *(Also known as PENNY'S and ADAM'S LEAP)*. On to what I like to call CATHEDRAL ROCK, if only there was access to fish this cove on to the clean patch of sand. Carry on to the famous GREEN BRIDGE of WALES.

Cathedral Rocks, St. Govans.

Venue 1: Newquay Cove (NGR 97.5 /93.1)

Walk to the left Eastwards towards the coastguard look out station across TREVALLEN Downs. After the gate, follow the tarmac road around to the left, and at the second concrete bunker turn left on to a chipping covered road/path. Then bear right at the danger warning sign down through a small valley to NEWQUAY COVE. *NB: Do not walk straight on at this point or you will miss the small hidden cove.*

The Cove is 25 yards wide at it's widest narrowing back to 7 yards in width. Small amounts of LAVER WEED on the stones in the sand on the left, with undersize Mussels on the rocks.

Try to arrive at bottom water to fish the mouth of the cove, and as the tide hems you retreat up on to the rocks nearest MATHEW Point casting out into the bay onto clean sand.

Try float fishing into the cove with Peeler Crab or live Sandeel for Bass.

If you have youngsters with you, keep an eye on them around this area, the cliffs are 160 Foot above sea level.

St. Govans Chapel, St. Govans.

Venue 2: Chapel Point (NGR 96.8 / 92)

ST. GOVANS CHAPEL is directly in front of the car park, leading down to it by some 74 irregular steps. The Chapel is built across an opening in the rocks and consisting of a single room measuring roughly 18 foot by 12 foot, and a further 32 Steps down to the Well, supposedly with healing qualities, but now dry, but further down is a small trickle of rust coloured water!

In the year 1662 it was known as 'ST. GOBINS WELL'. And the Chapel a Hermits Cell dating from either the 11th or 13th century. Is there a Silver Bell hidden in the Cliff nearby?

No firing on the Castle Martin range at the weekends or Bank Holiday. Mid week the sign on the left hand side of the road after ST. GOVANS INN indicates if the range road is open or closed. The firing times are on the notice board outside the café at BOSHERTON.

And finally we reach our last venue. Bottom water Spring Tides.

After parking walk down through the Chapel picking your way carefully with stout walking boots down towards the right to fish off the flat rocks at bottom water, casting out over the Kelp beds, with the Inland Stack Rock behind you. Expect heavy tackle losses.

NB: This venue is only for the foolhardy, not recommended, rough swirling waves have swept unwary anglers off the flat seaweed covered rocks, so be warned.

There is an emergency telephone at the Coastguard look out station on the headland, half a mile from the car park.
Number CASTLEMARTIN
01646 235

Footnote: In 1960 the headland was renamed from ST. GOWAN to ST. GOVANS.

Healing Well, St. Govans.

Supplementary Notes

Sea Weeds

Prior to eating, as our sea water is not always in pristine condition, soak in fresh clean tap water with a small quantity of the dark crystals of POTASSIUM PERMANGANATE for half an hour, then thoroughly wash out in cold water, the crystals will remove all the unsavoury aquatic organisms. The crystals can be obtained from the chemists in a small container. Just a small quantity required to turn the water purple.

Laverweed (Laverbread) – *"Porphyra Umbilicalis"*

Sea Laver is picked off the rocks towards bottom water, it is the black seaweed stuck flat to the rocks, you can feel it peeling off the stones when collecting.

To Prepare: Thoroughly clean, using the crystals and finish off by running under the cold tap. With the weed in a colander cut up small with a scissors, and cook in small batches, unless you have a large cooking utensil. *(NB: Take care if you try and mince in a food processor, it tends to burn out the motor, so be warned – I know!)*

Cooking: Rub the inside of a large saucepan with margarine, place in the Laver with a small quantity of water and bring to the boil, turn down the heat and simmer. Add more hot water when required to stop the weed and saucepan burning. After about one hour start adding slowly the seasoning, Pepper and Vinegar and very – very careful with the salt. Continue simmering for about another two hours adding seasoning to your taste. But remember to watch that the Laverbread does not stick to the pan and burn. It will finally turn to a thick paste like substance.

Samphire

The Sea Asparagus, two types: Marsh and Rock.

To prepare Marsh Samphire: Use the crystals to clean and remove any sand/grit particles. Cut off the rough part of the stem. Blanch quickly in hot water to remove some of the salty taste, then fry lightly in olive oil butter, but experiment.

When collecting cut with a scissors or shears just above the sand/mud to leave the roots intact.

92

Shell Fish, Eel & Shrimp

Crab

After collecting bring the Crab home alive by wrapping them individually in a damp saltwater cloth, then place in your bag or rucksack. Please only bring a couple of the larger ones home.

Cooking: No Condiments, season to taste after. Bring a large saucepan of water to the boil, and just before immersing the Crab into the boiling water, for humane reasons kill the Crab by lifting the tail flap and inserting the point of a clean baiting needle or skewer into the body. The cooking time for any size Crab is 20 to 25 Minutes, let the Crab cool naturally, then break off the claws cracking them open with a 'Toffee Hammer' taking care when extracting the white meat that all the shell is removed. Prise the top shell from the body, discard the two sets of five finger grey gills *(Dead Man's Fingers)* and the small stomach sac, which is usually left behind in the top shell behind the eyes. All the rest is edible. No poisonous parts in the Crab, but the Grey Gills are unedible – they taste horrible!

When you get to this stage, practice, patience and experience will determine how much white Crab meat can be extracted with a skewer or better still, with wooden barbecue kebab skewers from the claws and the honeycomb body section.

Mix some bread crumbs with a selection of herbs of your choice, Chives, Onions, Shallots, Garlic etc. Into this mixture place the soft brown Crab meat, mix together and place to one side of the cleaned top Crab shell, place the white Crab meat on the other side and cover with cling film.

Crab meat freezes well.

Cockles

Collecting: Cockles are found just below the sand surface, to collect, you need a small hand rake, sieve, and a onion type sack. I wear chest waders so I can kneel down to rake them up, be careful not to tear them on the shells.

The minimum size are between 17.5mm to 19mm, approximately $3/4$ of an inch. *(See my gauge drawing - page 123).*

When you find a Cockle bed kneel down and use the rake to

remove the Cockles from the sand into a pile and place the Cockles & mud/sand into the sieve, you will usually find a pool of sea water to riddle the Cockles clean. There is a legal limit on the amount you can take, so just take enough to cook in one session.

Cooking: When you get the Cockles home, tip them into a bucket and with the garden hose pipe wash the Cockles stirring continuously with your hands, until the water comes back to clean. Into a large saucepan place some tap water, *(without salt)* tip in a couple of handfuls of the Cockles so that the water is just covering them, bring to the boil and as soon as the water comes up to the boil and the Cockle shells open, they are cooked. Tip them into a colander and run under a cold tap until cool, then separate the Cockles from the shell.

Now comes the best part, the Cockles are full of the black gritty muck that all the books say before cooking, soak overnight in salt or Porridge Oats! to clean before cooking.

My Recipe: Use your clean hands to squeeze the Cockles whilst running under the cold tap with them still in the colander, keep squeezing lightly until they are completely free of grit and clean. Not an ounce of salt used from collecting to the plate, completely fresh. Now you can season to taste.

You can tell the age of a Cockle by the number of rings on the shell. Two the first year, then one every other year.

Some types of Cockle: QUEENS, STUKY BLUES and the juvenile known as SPATS. The name of the common Cockle is CARDRUM EDULE.

MUSSELS
Can be found on the rocks over a large area of Pembrokeshire, do not be surprised when you find small Red Striped Crabs living happily inside some of the larger Mussels.

You have seen Mussels being cooked on television then being eaten straight out of the shell. I would suggest a word of caution here, the difference between Farmed and Wild Mussels. The Farmed have been scrubbed clean .The hair that grips the wild Mussel to the rocks *(The Byssus)* goes through the shell and into the Mussels body, which should be removed after cooking – unmistakable.

Wash the Mussels clean in a bucket of cold water.

Cooking: In a large saucepan just cover the shells with cold water *(no salt)* and bring to the boil, the shells will have opened and the Mussel will be cooked. If the shell is still closed or damaged – discard. Run under the cold tap in a colander and remove the Mussel from the shell, check every one and remove the BYSSUS hair. Leave to rest in the fridge with herbs and condiments of your choice.

Winkles

Thoroughly wash the Winkles in a sieve, place the shells in a saucepan and just cover with water *(no salt)* and bring to the boil, turn down the heat and just simmer for about five minutes, the longer you leave them cooking the tougher they become.

Extract the snail from the shell with a pin or similar implement, then cut off the snails brown 'DOOR' with a scissors. Place the shelled snails in a bowl and sprinkle with Pepper and Vinegar.

Small Conger Eel

Try cooking by cutting the Eel into cutlet type pieces, and skin them separately, or simply bar boil to loosen the skin. Bake or fry.

The thick end of the EEL is best, the tail section is very bony.

Shrimps

Do not linger after collecting your Shrimps, because they need to be cooked as soon as possible, keep cool with freezer packs in your container whilst returning home.

Boil the Shrimps for about two to three minutes, they will float to the surface and are cooked *(no salt)*. Allow to cool, peel, chill in the fridge, or eat straight away.

Not a good freezer.

Baits

Let me try and give you a rough guide to baits for the more popular of species.

Bass: Crab, live Sandeel.

Bream: Long thin slices of Squid, Sand Eel, Fish Strips, Mudworm, Lugworm, Mussel, Soft section of Limpet. A real mixture of baits.

Brill: Sand Eel, Sprat, Pouting. All Fish baits.

Cod: Black Lugworm, Squid, Peeler Crab, Strips of Fish.

Conger Eel: Essential to use FRESH Fish baits. Squid, Mackerel etc. they like their food soft so pulp it up, and bind on with elasticated cotton.

Dab: Lugworm, Small Ragworm (Mudworm)

Dogfish: Fish Strips, Ragworm.

Flounder: Soft and Peeler Crab, Mudworm, Lugworm, Mackerel Strips, Mussel, Cockle, Venus Clams.

Garfish: Fresh and Frozen Sandeel. Ragworm, Thin strips of Mackerel.

Mackerel: Feathers, buy the better type.

Mullet: Bread Paste, Mudworm, Bread Flake, Brown Tip of the Tail of the Whelk.

Pollack: Try a wide variety of Fish and Worm baits. Hermit Crab Fresh or Frozen.

Ray Family: Bottom Feeders – so try Crab, Frozen Fish, and Worm baits.

Turbot: Live Greater Sandeel. Long fillet (Lask) if obtainable of an Eel.

Whiting: Lugworm, Ragworm, Mackerel, or Herring cut into thin strips.

Wrasse: This is where you can try the unusual baits: Limpets, Hard Backed Crab. Also any live bait you can find amongst the rocks.

Baits: Keeping and Storing.

Lugworm *(Types of Lugworm: Black, Yellow Tail & Blow).*

Black Lugworm: Along with your Bait Pump, take along a plastic bottle to bring home some clean sea water. Separate all the Broken and dead worms when you arrive home. Squeezing out the innards and set aside. *(See damaged worms).*

Into a large cat litter type tray pour a little of the clean sea water that you brought home in the plastic bottle, just enough to cover the bottom, place the whole undamaged worms into the tray and watch the ones that go into a coil, the ones that do not coil – gut and place with the other separated worms. You will have to keep changing the sea water and keep the tray clean, any worms extruding blood, set aside. The worms must be kept cool at all times, but not frozen, the colder months of the year will not be a problem, use freezer packs beneath the tray or inside with the worms, with the packs wrapped in clean bags. After a period of time depending on conditions etc., the worms will start to straighten it's time to use or gut.

Check the conditions of worms before buying, if in doubt, do not buy, they are not cheap to buy these days.

Damaged Black Lugworm and Yellow Tails: On the beach, nip off the head and gently squeeze from tail to head to remove the innards, wash the worms clean in sea water. These are kept separate from the whole undamaged live worms.

Buy a bag of pet shop sawdust which has no additives. Into a container place a couple of handfuls of cheap cooking Salt, *(about 25p a bag)* and a equal amount of sawdust, place the gutted worms into this mixture, and mix thoroughly. Place 8 to 10 worms into a small plastic bag, the ones with a self sealing end preferably – deep freeze.

Blow Lugworm: A difficult bait to keep, especially in the Summer months, they MUST be kept cool. Bring some clean sea water home with you, pour a small amount into a clean cat litter type tray, swill it around and then tip it all out to leave just a film of sea water. Carefully place the Lugworm into the tray. Discard or separate the damaged worms because they lose COELOMIC fluid and blood, this fluid in contact with good worms within a short period of time will destroy the lot, especially again if not kept cool. Wrap a frozen freezer pack in a clean plastic bag and place alongside the worms. Keep repeating this process. Without a fridge find the coldest place around your property, keep the tray clean removing any stains.

Remember, when digging Lugworm off the beach popular with visitors to the area, please Backfill the holes to prevent any accidents to the youngsters who might be just paddling in the incoming tide.

Years Ago
1903: A stone of Lugworm (14lbs), approximately 400 Worms cost 10 Shillings (50p). You would get around 40 Worms for one shilling and tupence (6p).

2003: 40 to 60 worms for £12. Around 5 worms approximately for a £1. A stone of Lugworm (14lbs), average of 50 Worms to the pound (lb), 400 Worms would cost you around £96!

What will they cost in 2103, if there are any left?

Razor Fish
At bottom water on a spring tide, walk along the sea shore and look for 'KEYHOLE' type holes in the sand. Take with you a container of household salt but NOT rock salt, and a squeegee bottle. Pour some salt into the bottle and fill with sea water, shake to mix. This can be squeezed into a series of holes, alternatively, pour neat salt into the holes, leave for a few minutes and watch for the Razor Fish shell pop up out of the sand.

As you walk along the sand you will sometimes see a spurt/jet of sea water coming out of the 'KEYHOLE'.

Grip the shell firmly and lift out of the hole slowly, do not snatch or you will be left with just the shell in your hand and the soft flesh of the fish left behind. Razor Fish Shells are sharp so take care. Please only take enough for the days fishing. Razor Fish are best used fresh, not such a good bait frozen, other than perhaps to tip off other baits such as Lugworm.

If you must freeze, wrap in bundles of five in kitchen foil and then greaseproof paper, place into freezer type bags and straight into the freezer. Our stocks of Razor Fish around Pembrokeshire are being decimated, so please again do not take a bucketful to freeze down, and then not use.

THINK OF THE FUTURE.

Razor Fish Spear

Making and using a Razor Fish Spear.

Obtain a length of $^3/_8$ inch round bar over and above 24" up to 36" in length, the longer the better. With a POWER SAW blade, which is about a inch wide, grind it down to about $^1/_2$" wide by 3" long. Grind it into a spear shape with two nicks, fit into a slot that has been cut into the round bar. It must be Brazed into position.

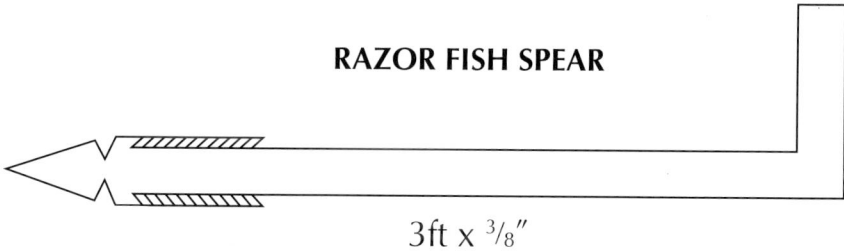

RAZOR FISH SPEAR

3ft x $^3/_8$"

To use: Push the spear down into the 'KEYHOLE' until you feel the shell, just push into the shell which will (or should) be open, twist a half turn and lift out the Razor Fish slowly. You will get the hang of it with practice.

Crab

Please for humane reasons kill the crab first before baiting up, to do so, stab under the tail flap or 'APRON'.

The simplest method of baiting up is to remove a back leg, insert the hook into the socket and out through the top shell, secure with elasticated cotton. But there are better ways.

Baiting Up:

'SAUSAGE' method for Peeler Crab. Completely strip the crab down

by removing all the legs and shell, and by cutting off the grey gills (*Dead Mans Fingers*) with a scissors until you are left with a lovely soft crab. If it is a reasonably sized crab, use the claws and legs to add to the hook point, or to tip off your other baits.

Do not penetrate the crab with the hook, loss of juices are too quick, just lay the crab along the shank of the hook rolled into a sausage shape, and if it is a small Peeler use two back to back. Whip on with thin elasticated cotton and leave all the hook showing.

Soft Crab: There is no need to strip the crab down, but I like to create a sausage like effect with the crab intact, then bait up as per Peeler.

'LOOP' method. (See Trace Drawing)
Mainly with soft crab, close range double or treble hook fishing off the rocks. Use a 18" to 20" Snood with a loop formed in the end, bend a piece of very fine wire into a tight 'U' shape, thread through the eye of the hook and push up through the underside of the Crab, now pull up slowly through the Crab, remove the wire. Push the loop of the line through the eye of the hook and over the Crab to secure. I use this method because the eye of the hook is still quite large, and will cause less break up of the Crab.

LOOPED CRAB RIG
for whole soft Crab close range

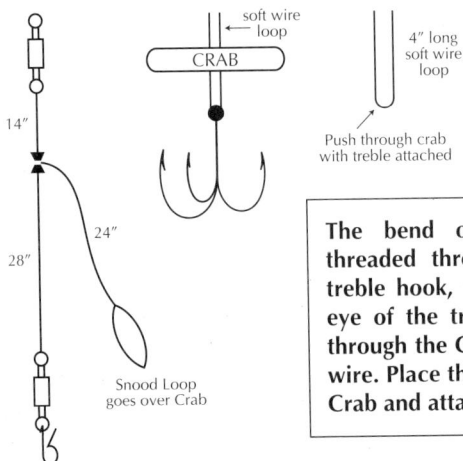

soft wire loop

CRAB

4" long soft wire loop

Push through crab with treble attached

14"

24"

28"

Snood Loop goes over Crab

The bend of the soft wire is threaded through the eye of the treble hook, this enables the large eye of the treble to be pulled up through the Crab. Then remove the wire. Place the Snood loop over the Crab and attach to the treble.

100

Without the use of a fridge, Soft Crab is a difficult bait to keep fresh for any length of time, but Peeler Crab can be kept alive for several days somewhere cool outside in a wooden or polystyrene type container. Place a couple of freezer packs into the container/box then some CLEAN sacking type material DAMPED with sea water on top of the cold packs. Place in the Peeler Crab and cover with another layer of damp sea water Sacking. Check every day and the 'POPPED' Crabs should be used or stripped down and frozen.

When you go collecting Crab, take a small garden spray bottle to fill with clean sea water to give them a quick spray each day.

Hermit Crab: Difficult Crab to find, but my favourite Bass bait. Not easy to extract from the shell, you cannot prise them out, and by cracking the shell you damage the very delicate Crab. So warm the shell with a match or lighter – out pops the Crab.

Preserving Crab: I've tried them all, but they have proved to be hopeless, so do not be fooled if you see any of these recipes, they are on a par with those artificial baits you see in small plastic bags in some tackle shops.

Ragworm *(Types of Ragworm: King, Harbour, White & Orange).*
Can I suggest three ways of keeping Harbour Mudworm *(there are other names throughout the country for the small delicate worm).*

Number 1: Materials required: Polystyrene box with lid *(the size of mine is 16" x 11" x 6", obtainable from Vegetable or Fish Merchants)*, six blue freezer packs and Potato Sacking.

Method: Place three of the frozen packs at the bottom of the box, cover with a double layer of just damp sea water sacking *(you will have to wash and clean the sacking first, even taking it with you fishing to leave it soak in the sea)*, when it has almost dried out it is ready to accept the worms.

When you bring the worms home, place them onto newspaper (not the coloured pages) to semi dry them and to remove most of the mud. Change the paper a number of times. Place the worms on top of the sacking inside the box. Spreading them out, cover with another layer of sacking, fit the lid in position and keep cool. Every day change the freezer packs with another three frozen ones, and check the worms.

Number 2: After bringing the worms home lay them on to sheets of newspaper for an hour or so to partially dry them out, and to separate from the mud.

Into a deep cat litter type tray, place thick layers of crushed SEA PEAT, tip the worms in and gently mix through, make the peat level, and lay a damp clean cloth on top.

Keep checking the worms daily, and if you think they need a bit of a boost, spray lightly with sea water. Experience and trial will determine how dry the peat should be, but keep them cool.

Number 3: To keep the worm for a short period of time. Lay the worm onto newspaper to dry out, change the paper a number of times, do not leave the worms in wet paper – a sure fire killer of the worms. Mix the dry worms with crushed/shredded almost dry SEA PEAT.

When using Mudworm for Flounder, tip off the bait with a thin strip of Mackerel roughly $1/2$ inch by about 2 inches in length. Cut the Mackerel into rings.

Preparing Sea Peat: When you find a large 'BALL' of Sea Peat on the beach drop it in a bag as it is, and when you get home cut off the outer edges, like removing crusts of bread to leave the more pure clean peat. Leave to dry out somewhat and then crumble just enough to mix with the worms. Leave the rest of the peat whole.

Squid

Buy a box of CALARMARI SQUID and keep frozen until the day before fishing, then gradually unfreeze until you can remove a couple of the Squid, then refreeze the rest. Slice the skin into strips to hang on the hook with another bait. Also use the head tentacles.

Baits: Homemade Pastes

When you prepare your tackle box and bait, take two boxes for your bait. One to leave in the dry, out of the sun, rain or spillage and just take a few at a time to put into the other bait bucket to hang onto the rod rest.

Beach Rubby Dubby

> *Materials:* Coarse Swimfeeder.
> 2 ounce Bomb Weight.
> Sea Peat.
> Cat Litter Tray.
> Jam Jar with Lid

Method: After collecting a mixture of baits *(Worm, Cockle, Lug, Clams, Razor)*, open the shelled bait over a cat litter type tray to catch the liquid, and any broken/damaged or surplus baits drop into the tray. Grind up the peat and mix with the juice and bait in the tray. Place in a jam jar and seal.

At the beach, place a 1 ounce or 2 ounce weight into the Swimfeeder, mix in your *Rubby Dubby* with some small live bait, no need to cast any distance.

If you have insufficient Rubby Dubby take some peat and another jam jar to the beach and a small plastic sheet to make up some more, you will always find some sort of bait on the beach.

Mullet Bread Paste

Remove the crust from a loaf of bread and make up some bread crumbs, put half to one side and thoroughly wet the other half with sea water, squeeze out the excessive moisture, now mix in the dry bread crumbs until the correct texture is obtained, smooth and slightly sticky. Mix with crushed clean small ragworm.

Prepare bait at home, wrap in cling film and take plenty of dry breadcrumbs to mix into the moist mixture.

Holiday Bait

> *Materials:* Coleman Cooler Box.
> 8 Corks, ask for them at your local pub or club.

Blue Freezer Pack.
Small plastic food box with a tight fitting lid.

Method: With *Araldite,* stick the corks together in twos, then stick them to the DRY base of the cooler box.

On the bottom go the Ragworm mixed with peat, next the freezer pack wrapped in a plastic type freezer bag, this is placed on top of the corks. Then the small plastic box on top of the freezer pack with the Lugworm inside, the box is just moistened with sea water, make sure the lid is fitted tightly, even binding with electrical tape. Peeler Crab are then jammed down the sides, and the whole lot is sealed tightly with moistened sea watered newspaper

HOLIDAY BAIT COOLER BOX

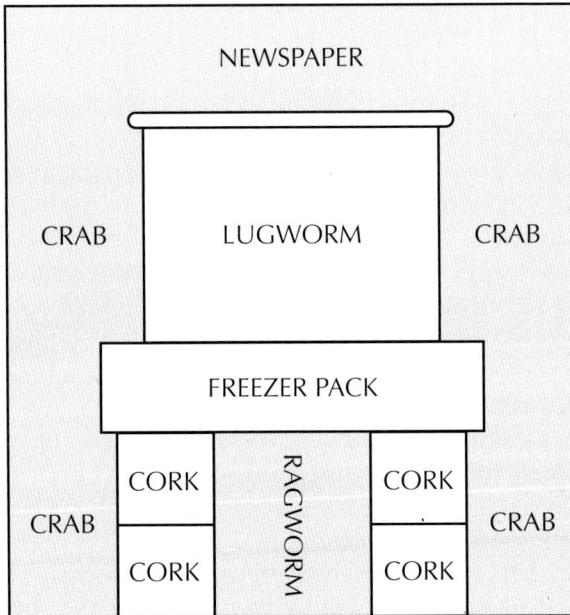

Knots

Try and learn to tie these simple knots for trace making. There are numerous knot books on the market.

1. Most Important: Shock Leader

2. To Swivels and Hooks: Half Tucked Blood

3. For stand off snoods: Blood or Dropper

4. Loops for rotten bottom: Figure 8 Loop or 5 Tucked Loop

5. Sliding Floats: Sliding Stop Knot

6. Barrel Knot: Stop Knot

7. Double Slip Knot: Line to Reel Spool

Hook Anatomy

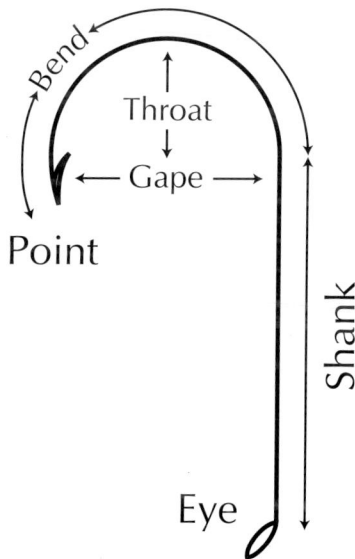

2 Hook Crab Beater

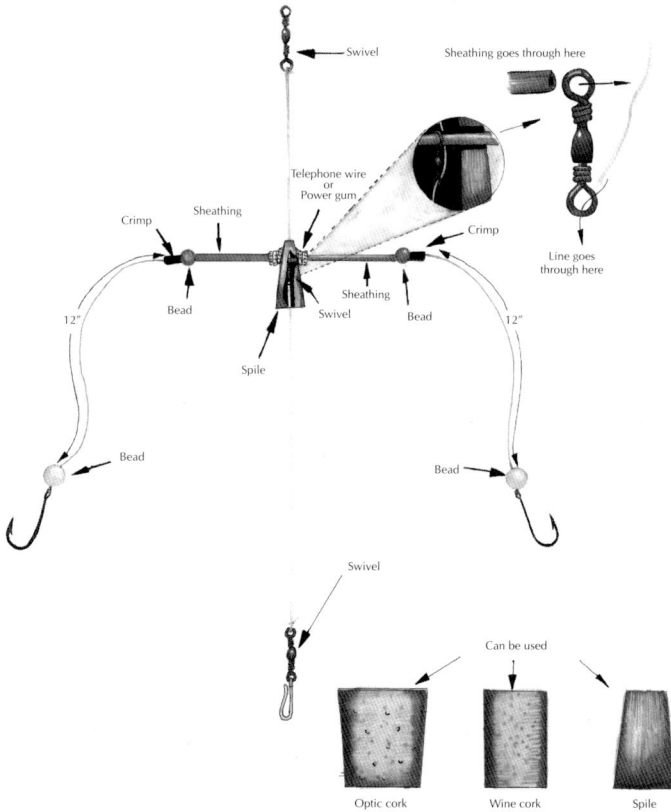

Swivel

Sheathing goes through here

Telephone wire or Power gum

Crimp

Sheathing

Crimp

Line goes through here

12"

Bead

Sheathing

Swivel

Bead

12"

Spile

Bead

Bead

Swivel

Can be used

Optic cork

Wine cork

Spile

Materials used

5" Electrical Sheathing	4 Beads – 2 of 5mm
3 Swivels – 2 x size 6	2 of 8mm
1 x size 8	50lb Shock Leader
Telephone wire or power gum	20lb Amnesia Snood
2 Crimps	1 Genie Linkclip
	2 Hooks

Clipped Pulley

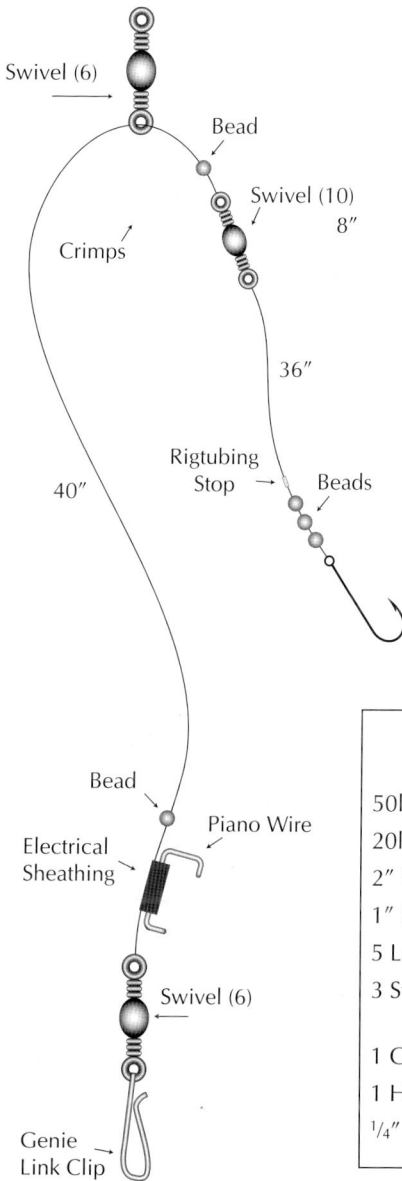

Swivel (6)

Bead

Swivel (10)

8"

Crimps

36"

40"

Rigtubing
Stop → Beads

Bead

Electrical
Sheathing

Piano Wire

Swivel (6)

Genie
Link Clip

Materials used

50lbs Shock Leader

20lbs Amnesia Snood

2" Piano Wire

1" Electrical Sheathing

5 Luminous 5mm Beads

3 Swivels – 2 x size 6
1 x size 10

1 Genie Link Clip

1 Hook

$1/4$" Rig Tubing Stop Knot

Rotten Bottom

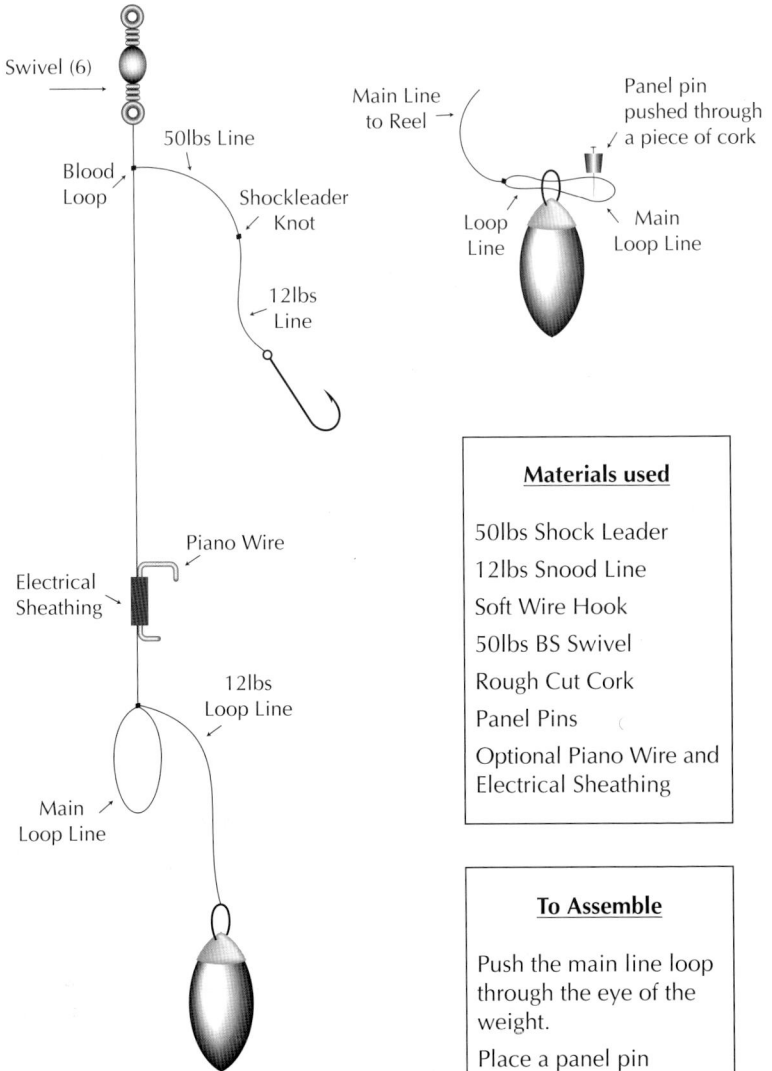

Swivel (6)

50lbs Line

Blood Loop

Shockleader Knot

Main Line to Reel →

Panel pin pushed through a piece of cork

Loop Line

Main Loop Line

12lbs Line

Piano Wire

Electrical Sheathing

12lbs Loop Line

Main Loop Line

Materials used

50lbs Shock Leader

12lbs Snood Line

Soft Wire Hook

50lbs BS Swivel

Rough Cut Cork

Panel Pins

Optional Piano Wire and Electrical Sheathing

To Assemble

Push the main line loop through the eye of the weight.

Place a panel pin through the loop of the main line.

Keep tight when casting

Clipped Lead Beach Bomb

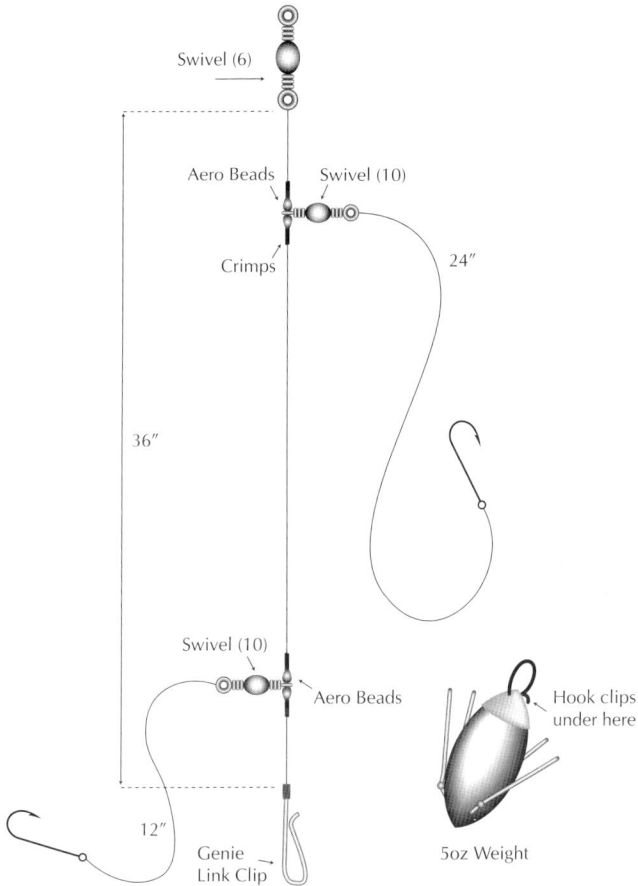

Swivel (6)

Aero Beads   Swivel (10)

Crimps

24″

36″

Swivel (10)

Aero Beads   Hook clips under here

12″

Genie Link Clip   5oz Weight

Materials used

3 Swivels – 1 x size 6, 2 x size 10	2 Hooks
1 Genie Link Clip	50lbs Shock Leader
4 Crimps	20lbs Amnesia Snood
4Aero Beads	5oz Clipped Lead

Clipped Pennell

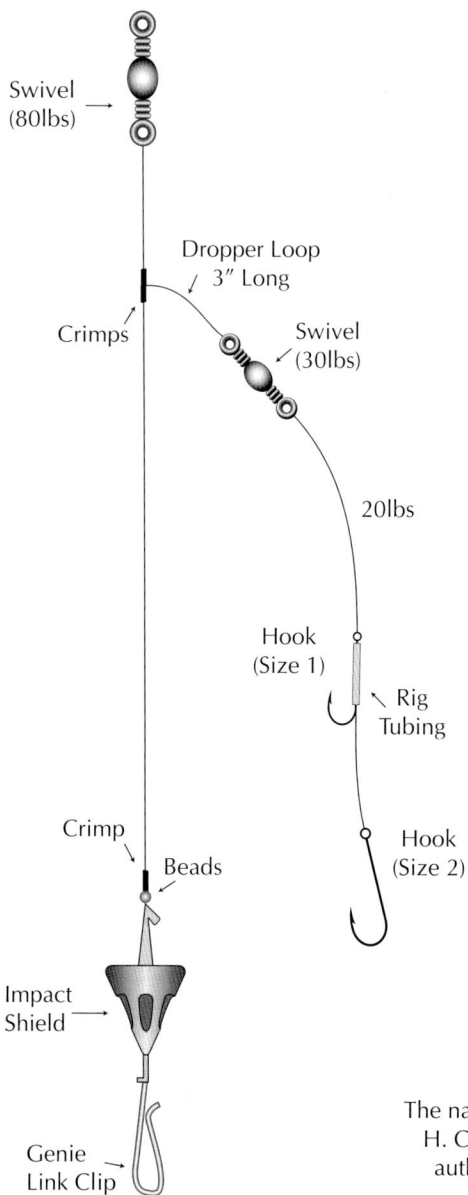

Swivel
(80lbs) →

Knots

Dropper Loop
Half Tucked Blood

Dropper Loop
/ 3″ Long

Crimps

Swivel
/ (30lbs)

Materials used

50lbs Mainline
20lbs Snoodline
2 Hooks – 1 x size 1
1 x size 2
1 Genie Link Clip
1 Breakaway Impact
Shield
2 Swivels – 1 x 80lbs
1 x 30lbs
1 5mm Bead
2 Crimps
2″ Rig Tubing

20lbs

Hook
(Size 1)

Rig
Tubing

Crimp

Beads

Hook
(Size 2)

Impact
Shield →

The name PENNELL named, after
H. C. Pennell. A 19th century
author and designer of rigs.

Genie
Link Clip

110

Flounder Rig
One hook below, one hook above

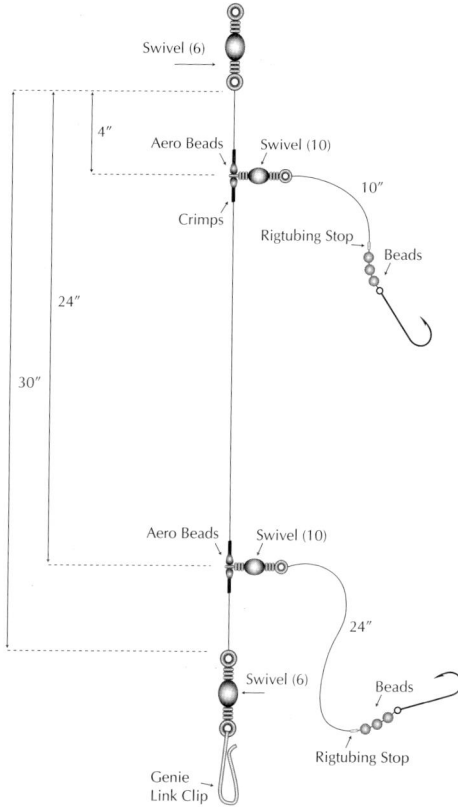

Swivel (6)

4"

Aero Beads

Swivel (10)

10"

Crimps

Rigtubing Stop

Beads

24"

30"

Aero Beads

Swivel (10)

24"

Swivel (6)

Beads

Rigtubing Stop

Genie
Link Clip

Materials used

4 Swivels –
(2 x size 6, 2 x size 8)

1 Genie Link Clip

4 Crimps

4 Aero Beads

2 Hooks

50lbs Shock Leader

20lbs Amnesia Snood

6 x 8mm Beads

$1/4$" Rig Tubing Stop

3 Hook Running Paternoster

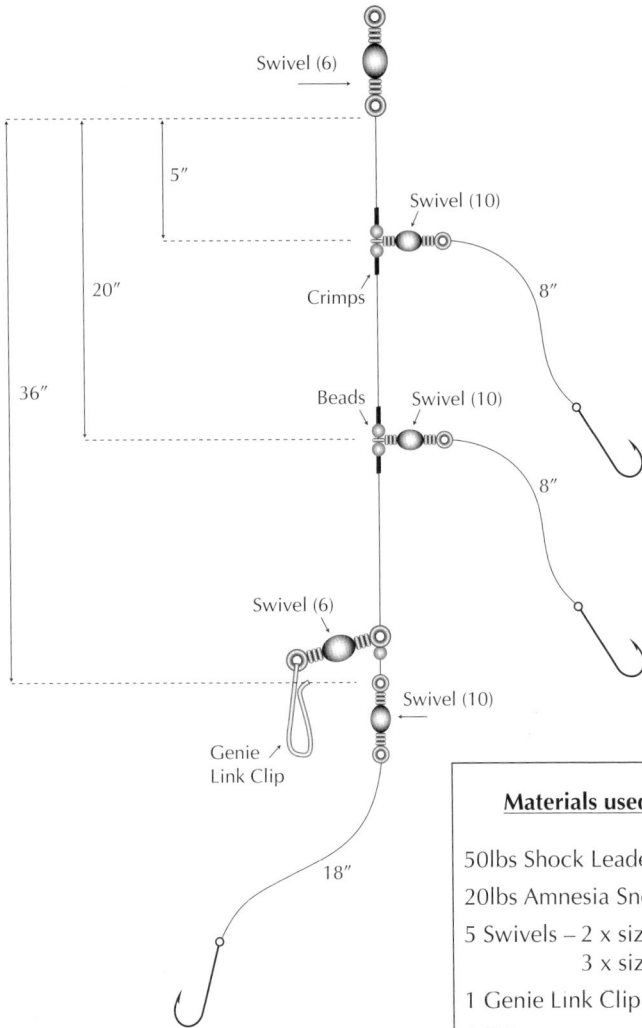

Swivel (6)

5″

Swivel (10)

20″

Crimps

8″

36″

Beads   Swivel (10)

8″

Swivel (6)

Genie
Link Clip

Swivel (10)

18″

Materials used

50lbs Shock Leader

20lbs Amnesia Snood

5 Swivels – 2 x size 6
3 x size 10

1 Genie Lınk Clip

4 Crimps

5 x 5mm Beads

3 Hooks

Flonder Rig Hooks Above

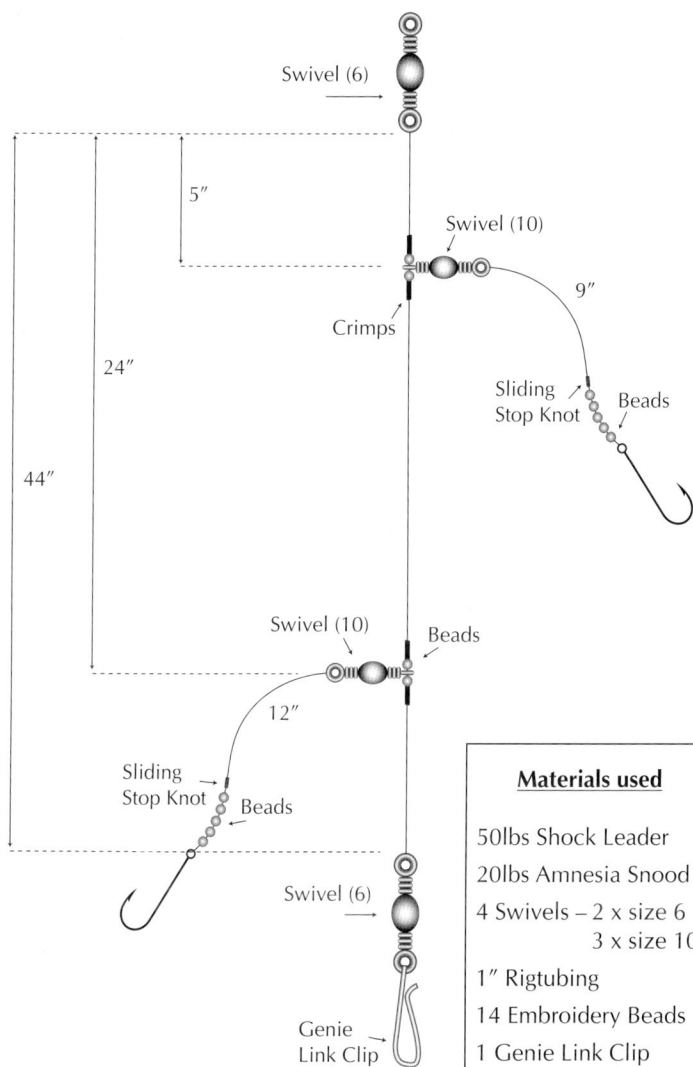

Swivel (6)

5"

Swivel (10)

9"

Crimps

24"

Sliding
Stop Knot   Beads

44"

Swivel (10)   Beads

12"

Sliding
Stop Knot   Beads

Swivel (6)

Genie
Link Clip

Materials used

50lbs Shock Leader

20lbs Amnesia Snood

4 Swivels – 2 x size 6
            3 x size 10

1" Rigtubing

14 Embroidery Beads

1 Genie Link Clip

4 Crimps

2 Hooks

Swivels

Having tested most of the Swivels on to days market, I have found that NONE actually swivel under the smallest of load strain, they are basically attachments for today's market. For a Swivel to turn under load would be too expensive, needing a ball bearing type set up.

'Am I wrong?' Try your own test as follows:

SWIVEL TESTING

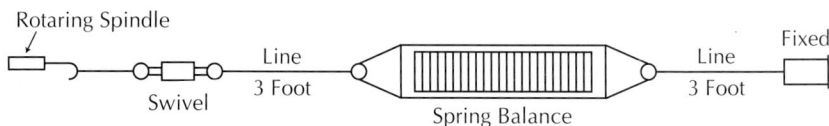

Try this set up, and turn the drill chuck as slowly as possible, with the slightest of pressure on the spring balance – see what happens.

Can I also put forward the following suggestion, a so called 'Rolling Weight' will not roll in the tide. I believe when the fishing line enters the water the pull on the line from this point to the weight would be impossible for the round ball weight to roll, but is just pulled to the left or right depending on the condition and state of the tide.

Therefore, a Swivel will not swivel and a Ball Weight will not roll.

Agree or disagree?

Weight of a Round Fish without a scale

A Book by Eric Marshall Hardy called *Angling Ways – 10th Edition*, 1973, relates to 'MONA'S SCALE', first published in 1918. It is a PIKE scale with various lengths and weights. It starts with a Pike of 20", which will weigh $2^1/_2$ lbs – 40" will weigh 20 lbs and 60" will weigh $67^1/_2$ lbs. But it was suggested that a formula that measures the Length and Girth would be more accurate, this was in 1918.

Eighty-one years later in 1999, a book by Fernandez Roman entitled *Fisherman's Guide to Tackle* comes up with the following formula: Measure the Girth. Square the measurement. Multiply it by the Length. Then divide by 25.

$$(G^2 \times L \div 25)$$

But this is the one I like:
A Book by Charles Wade, 1977, *entitled Fishing with the Experts*, writes the following.

> *If you catch a fish too heavy to weigh on a small spring balance, cut down a long smooth branch, support one end on a large tree trunk, hang your fish in the middle, use the small spring balance at the other end of the branch, lift and multiply the reading by 2.*

Try it.

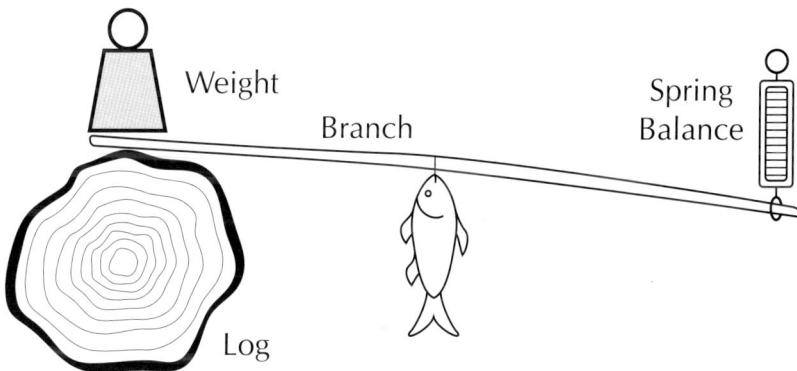

115

Rod Test Curves

Simple guide to test curves is to lay the rod on grass, run the line from the reel up through the eyes and tie off just below the tip ring *(Do not pull up through the tip ring eye).* Lock off the Star Drag on the reel, attach the end of the line to a spring balance and place your foot on the butt area of the rod, pull the spring balance until the rod tip is at right angles to the rod, read off on the spring balance scale.

Example of how to set up a test curve.

Alternatively, clamp the butt to a shed or wall, and pull off at right angles to read off the poundage on the spring balance. The more powerful beach rods will require a heavy duty spring balance with higher poundage readings.

This test curve will give you a rough guide to casting weights, although the makers allow some tolerances for mistakes whilst casting.

A 2lbs test curve allows 2 ounces of lead to be cast, and if you multiply the test curve by 5, you get a rough guide to breaking strain line.

Therefore, a 2lbs test curve equals 10lbs breaking strain line. To this add a shock leader of 20lbs.

4 ounce lead, minimum shock leader 40lbs breaking strain.

5 ounce lead, minimum shock leader 50lbs breaking strain.

Rod Tapers
Reverse Tapers: This is when the taper gets bigger from the Butt End up the rod, then tapers back down towards the tip end of the rod.

Fast Tapers: Tapers down throughout the whole length of the rod.

116

Star Drag Adjustment

The drag on the fishing reel is adjusted on the 'STAR WHEEL' inside the handle on the Multiplier Reel and on the Fixed Spool by the tensioning knob on the top or bottom whatever type of Fixed Spool Reel you use. So here is how to set it on the Multiplier, the principle is the same on the fixed spool:

Fit the reel to the rod and thread the line through the eyes and attach to a spring balance. A friend can now help by pulling the spring balance whilst you tension the Star Drag Wheel. The general rule of thumb is to set the drag to one third of the breaking strain of the line, therefore, on a 15 lbs breaking strain line set the drag to 5 lbs by slackening the Star Wheel right off. Mark one of the 'SPOKES' on the wheel and count how many turns it takes to get it to the 5 lbs setting on the Spring Balance. If you tighten the drag to 8 lbs, more than half the breaking strain of the line, you risk breakages.

It is nice to see the drag set correctly and start to slip.

Fixed Spool Reel – adjustable knob is at the front of the spool

Multiplier Reel – adjustable 'star wheel' is located at the side of the spool

117

Compass

Various types of compass to buy, but always buy one of good quality. Essential for boat fishing, and for beach fishing a handy piece of equipment to have, even if it is just to see which way the wind is blowing. East does not seem too popular.

Finding North: Hold the compass flat and away from Iron and Steel objects, the red needle will swing towards North, rotate the dial until the arrow is between the two luminous dots, you are now facing North.

Once the basics are grasped, all other readings can be developed/ learned and put into practice, especially during darkness and fog.

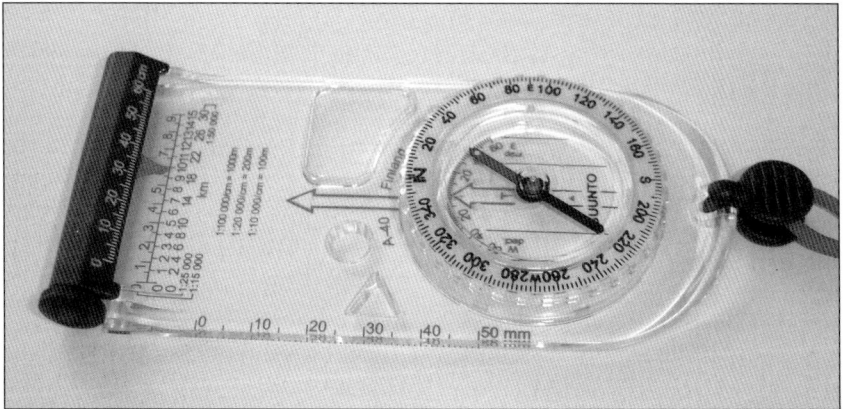

Never skimp on quality when buying a compass.

Map measurer – a handy piece of kit for calculating distances when reading from a map

Pedometer

Please buy a good quality Pedometer. Full instructions come with the instrument, mine has on the back a small slide adjuster to be set to your stride length. Right or wrong this is how I set mine up. With chalk measure out your stride length say over 20 paces – mark each step – I am 5 foot 10 inches tall and my stride length is just under the 24 inch stride mark. Now jump into your car and set the odometer to zero. Drive the car for one mile marking the start and finish points with chalk or whatever.

Now walk the mile that you drove in the car, with the pedometer hooked into your waist belt, check the accuracy and compare the both, it might need a couple of attempts to get the reading correct.

ROMAN NUMERALS:

1 = I	9 = IX	60 = LX
2 = II	10 = X	90 = XC
3 = III	11 = XI	100 = C
4 = IV	20 = XX	400 = CD
5 = V	30 = XXX	500 = D
6 = VI	40 = XL	900 = CM
7 = VII	50 = L	1000 = M
8 = VIII		

The older books were published using roman numerals for the year published. What year was this book published. MCMXL111?

Here are some clues?

$(C - M) = 900$
$(X - L) = 40$
$(I - X) = 9$
$(X - IX) = 19$
$(L + X) = 60$

Can you see how it works?

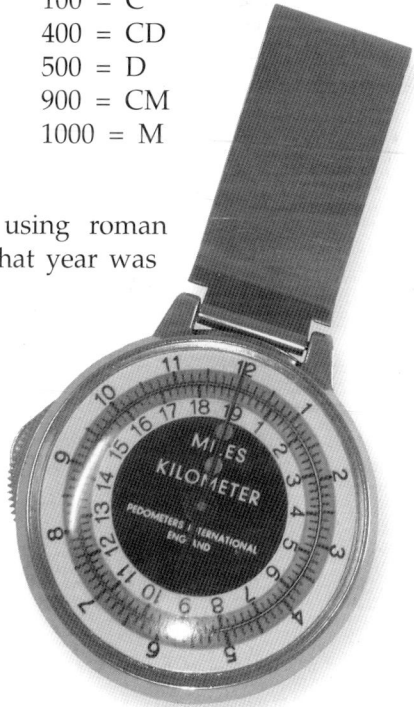

Length & Distance

1 mil = 0.0254 millimeter	1 Rod/Perch *(Surveyors Pole)* = 16.5 feet
1 inch = 2.54 centimeters	1 engineers chain = 100 feet
1 hand = 4 inches	1 football pitch = 100 yards
1 foot = 30.48 centimeters (12 inches)	1 furlong = 220 yards (201.17 meters)
1 pace = 2.5 feet	1 mile = 1.6093 kilometers
1 yard = 3 feet (0.914 meter)	1 nautical mile = 1.1515 mile
1 meter = 3.28 feet	1 league = 3 miles
1 fathom = 6 feet	1 marathon = 26.219 miles

Weights and Measures

Avoirdupois	Metric
$1/4$oz	7 grams
1oz	28.35 grams
2oz	57 grams
3oz	85 grams
4oz	113 grams
8oz	226 grams
1lb	454 grams (0.45kg)
$1^1/_2$lb	680 grams
2lb	907 grams (0.90kg)

Leader Breaking Strain

15lb	6810 grams (6.8kg)
25lb	11.3kg
35lb	15.8kg
40lb	18.1kg
45lb	20.4kg
50lb	22.7kg (22700 grams)

Minimum Fish Sizes

The minimum size limits prescribed for sea fish in this district are set out below – in centimetres:

Bass	37.5cm
Blue Ling	70.0cm
Cod	35.0cm
Grey Mullet	35.0cm
Haddock	30.0cm
Hake	27.0cm
Herring	20.0cm
Horse Mackerel (Scad)	15.0cm
Ling	63.0cm
Mackerel	20.0cm
Megrim	25.0cm
Plaice	27.0cm
Pollack	30.0cm
Red Mullet	15.0cm
Saithe	35.0cm

South Wales Sea Fisheries Commitee

Queens Buildings
Cambrian Place
Swansea. SA1 1TW

Tel: 01792 654466
Fax: 01792 645987
E.mail: SWSFC@aol.com

Skate and Ray	45.0cm	*Across wings*
" " "	22.0cm	*Single detached wing*
Sole	24.0cm	
Whiting	27.0cm	
Lobster	9.0cm	*Carapace length (max size pending)*
Nephrops	8.5cm	*Overall length (ICES VIIa 7.0cm)*
	4.6cm	*Tails (ICES VIIa 3.7cm)*
Edible Crab	14.0cm	*Across broad of back*
Velvet Crab	6.5cm	*Across broad of back, excluding spines*
Crawfish	11.0cm	*Carapace length*
Spider Crab	12.0cm	*Carapace length*
Scallop	11.0cm	*Across broad part of the flat shell*
Queen Scallop *(Chlamys spp)*	4.0cm	
Grooved Carpetshell *(Ruditapes decussatus)*	4.0cm	
Carpetshell *(Venerupis pullastra)*	3.8cm	
Short-necked Clam *(Ruditapes philippinarum)*	4.0cm	
Clam *(Venus verucosa)*	4.0cm	
Hard Clam *(Callista chione)*	6.0cm	
Razor Clam *(Ensis siliqua)*	10.0cm	
Surf Clam *(Spisula solidissima)*	2.5cm	
Donax Clams *(Donax spp)*	2.5cm	
Bean Solen *(Pharus legumen)*	6.5cm	

Periwinkle – Must not pass through square aperture of 13mm (0.5″)
Oyster – Must not pass through circular aperture of 51mm (2″) diameter
Cockle – Must not pass through square aperture of 19mm (³/₄″) – *unless by authorisation*
Mussel – In length 51mm (2″) – *unless by authorisation*
Whelk – Must not pass through square aperture of 35mm (1.38″) – *25mm by authorisation*

Lobster and Crab Gauge Guide

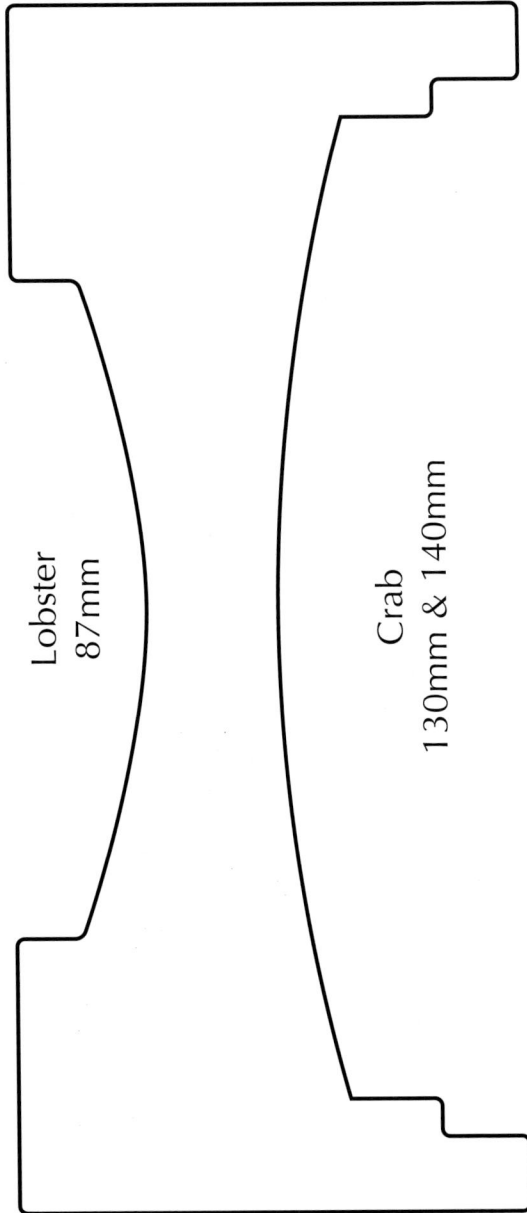

Lobster
87mm

Crab
130mm & 140mm

Multigauge
~ *Oyster, Cockle, Mussel, Winkle* ~

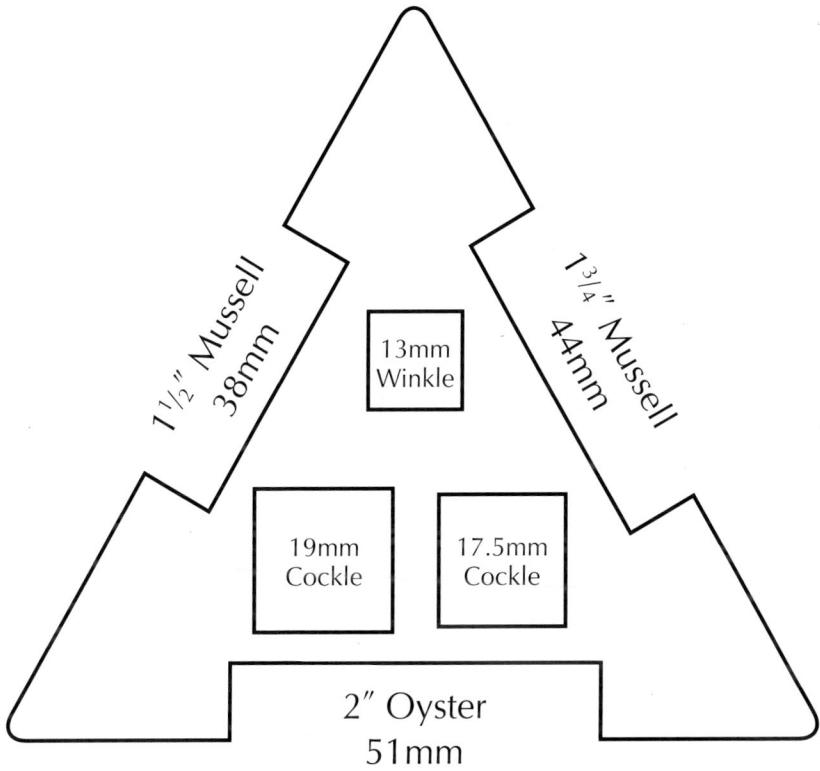

1½" Mussell 38mm

1¾" Mussell 44mm

13mm Winkle

19mm Cockle

17.5mm Cockle

2" Oyster 51mm

You can make templates off these gauges if of will help to preserve our stocks

Beach Barbecue

Materials: Barbecue Coals.

Silver Foil.

Firelighters.

Small Wire Mesh Grill
(size approximately 10" x 8" with 2" upstands).

Method: Dig a hole in the sand about 10" deep by approximately 8" in diameter, line with silver foil. Place in a good handful of coals mixed with firelighters onto the silver foil. Build a small shield/screen to keep off the wind with stones and sand. Light and cover with the grill. On completion dispose of the foil and backfill, leaving just the grill to take home.

BEACH BBQ

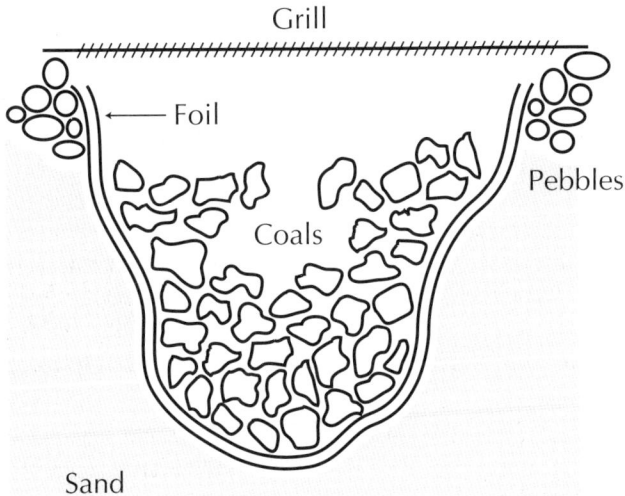

Children's Holiday Swimming Guide

One: Swim in the areas marked by RED and YELLOW Flags, and preferably patrolled by Lifeguards.

Two: Watch for warning signs, and swim in the middle of the beach.

Three: Do not swim with an empty stomach, and wait at least an hour after having a meal, just some safeguards against cramp.

Four: If you have bought them an inflatable floating device, make sure you also buy a length of rope to attach to it. You hold the other end on the sea shore, and please especially if the tide is going out.

Five: When they first enter the water, make sure they do not swim straight out, but swim in their depth along the beach until their body temperature matches the sea temperature.

Six: And finally – Supervise at all times, it matters not how good a swimmer they are, the sea is uncompromising.

Competition Fishing

Some suggestions for fishing a competition on an unknown beach which has sand, small shingle. Arrive well in advance (even the day before) just before bottom water to give yourself time to search. Look for any type of outfall pipe, or sewerage pipe, however small, if only a trickle of water, this is the favourite haunt of small sea creatures, shrimps, small crabs etc. Look for any part of the beach that looks different from the rest, an odd patch of seaweed anchored to the stones.

Sand/mud mixture, rivulets and small gullies, look for Flounder marks (indents in the sand), small rock pools, Mussel beds, Lugworm beds, etc.

Make a mental picture, so when the tide covers your mark you have an idea where to cast, the fish are not always out beyond the third wave, Bass and Flounder are sometimes under your feet when you walk out to cast. Yes, learn distance casting, it is an integral part of our sport, but also feel confident to cast short, you do not have to bomb the horizon every cast.

Another thing to think about is the shape of the beach, flat, steep, shelving, rocky, muddy, there are so many variants. GOOD LUCK.

Weaver Fish

Approximately 15cm long, lays buried just below the sand surface with just the stinging spine protruding above the sand and below the water, and if stepped on will give some considerable pain. If a Hospital is nearby a visit is recommended, but if not place the infected foot in **hot water** to help solidify the sting, keep changing the hot water until the pain subsides. Inform your GP after.

Take extreme care if you are unlucky enough to catch one, if you are unsure of your catch, cut the line just above the hook to leave the fish drop back into the sea. The hook will soon dissolve.

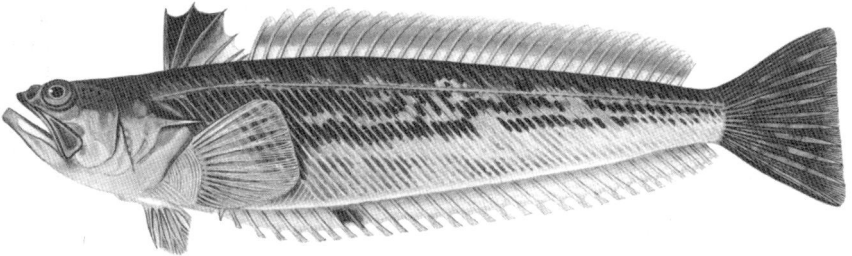

A book by H. MUIR EVANS on Sting Fishes dated 1943 (MCMXLIII) by FABER and FABER writes the following text from the 91st psalm:

"There shall no evil happen unto thee that thou hurt not thy foot against a stone, thou shalt go upon the LION and ADDER *(asp)* the young LION and the DRAGON shalt thou tread under thy feet)

Does this psalm refer to fish as Mr Evans implies?

Lion Fish: is also known as SCORPION FISH.
Adder: ADDER WEAVER or VIPER WEAVER.
Dragon Fish: or GREATER WEAVER.

Stones

Along the side of the roads throughout Pembrokeshire were stones originally called 'FINGER POSTS' for direction and distance, dating from 1694, sadly mostly all gone, just the odd Milestone left.

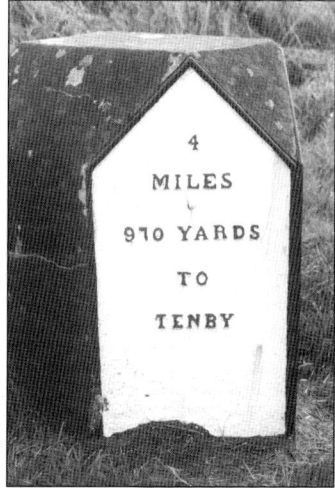

Milestone.

Cross: Or what I call 'OGHAM SCRIPT'. A Stone carved and marked on the sides as a memorial.

Dolmen: Upright stone and a Capstone.

Menhir: Single stone, ritual/religious.

Rubbing: This is the one I like, put up by farmers for their cattle to have a good scratch.

Inland Stack: Caused by subsidence.

Tor: Mainly granite weathered to look like a pile of stones.

Pudding: You will see these along our coastline, pebbles stuck together by natural cement.

Cairn: If you pile a load of stones on the beach to leave your mark, this is a basic cairn.

Rocking: How did they get there? A large stone balancing.

Trilithon: Two upright stones with a lid.

Henge: Circle of stones, still unsure how they were erected, where from, and the reason.

Erratic: A stone that is unfamiliar to it's source.

Jet: Very hard yet light in weight jet black pebble, burns with a greenish flame and pleasant smell.

Flaming Amber: Light coloured or yellowish soft pebble, burns with a yellow flame and sweet smell. *Valuable.*

Cromlechs: Prehistoric burial chamber, put up about 3000 BC. The men and women put the Capstone on by means of some sort of wooden rollers and levers. What were the hoist ropes made of? Weaved Grass?
    Capstones could weigh as much as 12 tons!

Useful and *Useless* information

When a wave breaks and creates a mass of foam it's called a 'WHITE CAP' and the shower of spray along the wave is called a 'SPINDRIFT'. Inside the curl of a wave is the 'GREEN ROOM'.

The term 'STORM BEACH' means the beach fishes well a couple of tides after a storm way offshore, and creates a good surf stirring up the bottom, forcing the worms, shells, Sand Eels, etc. from the sand.

When using a main line with a shock leader of say 50lbs breaking strain line. **Do not** use an American type snap swivel to support the weight, it could open under the strain of casting, they are only suitable for close range fishing.

It is possible to tell the age of a BASS by the number of rings on it's scales.

A simple Crabbing Hook: Bamboo cane, Allen key. Just push the Allen key into the narrow end of the cane secure with Araldite.

Flounder, Plaice, Dabs: When young, the eyes are on both sides of the head, but because the bone structure of it's skull develops unequal, one eye migrates to the top of it's head on the left hand side. But on the Turbot and Brill the other eye migrates to the right hand side.

Ballan Wrasse: All are born female, then after about 8 or 9 years, some decide to change to males.

The Eel: In the Larvae form it is a Flat Fish (LEPTOCEPHALUS) then 'ELVER' then 'BOOTLACE'. Look at the face of a Coconut!

First aid kit for youngsters: Bandages or clean cloths cut into strips (plasters are no use), electrical tape to bind. Cut the foot section off a sock to be able to pull up over the knee, wrap and seal in a Polythene bag. Rucksacks are not waterproof.

Learn to pack your Tackle Box in the same order every time you go fishing, it's surprising when you get to the venue the things you want to come out first seem to have gone down to the bottom of your tackle box/rucksack.

Bass: Question – Should we keep all the Bass below 15 inches in length? And put all the bigger Breeding Bass back. Or Photograph and put them all back.

Competition Fishing: Make up a spare trace ready to clip on. It's called 'Double Patting'

Trace Bag: Do not make up too many traces, if left in the plastic skin bags the hooks are the first to deteriorate. Four would be ample but if you must make-up more put a small amount of *rice* into the trace bag, unless fishing Rotten Bottom, or over Rocks where Tackle loses are high.

Ice Packs: Glycerine Filled

Skomer Island: Gradually the sea rose until 'NAB HEAD' became a coastal promontory, which means a point of high land jutting out into the sea. Separated from the mainland by the treacherous 'JACK SOUND'

Digging bait in the Winter and your hands are freezing. In SIBERIA the coldest place on earth is 'OIMYAKON' with temperatures dropping to as low as minus 97.8 F, breath freezes into crystals. . . Keep Digging!

Catching Mackerel for bait on the outgoing boat trip. The first Mackerel you catch, cut off the head, hook through the bottom jaw and cast in as soon as possible to get below the shoaling Mackerel. Bass below?

Two species of Seal breed in Britain, Common and Grey. Common are less than six foot long, round head and short front nose. Grey have a long head and pronounced nose.

Lobster: Has 3 stomachs, taste with their feet and can live to be 100.

Octopus: Has three hearts.

Shark: Can lose and replace up to 30,000 teeth during it's lifetime.

The French name for a fishing bell is 'GRELOT'

Balti: Means Bucket

White Stone: from the beach with Heather placed on top supposedly brings good luck.

To Convert Kilometres to Miles.

$$KM \frac{DISTANCE}{8} \times 5 = MILES$$

Found on the beach:
The egg mass of the Common Whelk, it's the whitish sponge type ball you see blowing around the beach.

Flat white shell of the CUTTLEFISH.

'MERMAIDS PURSE' flat plastic type square pockets with pointed corners. The Egg case of the Dogfish.

The White Shell and Stalk on old wood/crates etc. is the GOOSE BARNICLE.

If you are using a mixture of shell baits (*e.g. Cockle, Mussel, Clams etc.*) and opening them live on the beach, open them over a container to catch the liquid, then after baiting up a spare trace let it rest in the juices.

How does the tide go in and out?
Gravitational pull of the Moon and to a lesser degree that of the Sun on our Planet. The Moons pull is not strong enough to pull the water straight up, but strong enough to create a horizontal pull. So the water is pulled after the Moons rotation, causing the water to pill up on opposite sides of our planet to give *high tides*, and the other side where the water level has dropped *low tides*.

The Moon goes round our Planet once every 28 days. Whilst our planet revolves on it's Axis once every 24 hours – That's enough!

The FIXED SPOOL REEL came about around 1890 by Alfred Holden Illingworth. His idea came about possibly because he was working in the wool industry and as a keen fisherman transferred the spinning bobbing into the idea of the Fixed Spool Fishing Reel.

The MULTIPLYER REEL Invented in America by George Snyder of Kentucky in 1810. A Silversmith by profession in Paris, Kentucky. President of BOURBON County Anglers Association.

Islands

There are 31 islands of the coast of Wales, how many can you name?

1. ————————————————
2. ————————————————
3. ————————————————
4. ————————————————
5. ————————————————
6. ————————————————
7. ————————————————
8. ————————————————
9. ————————————————
10. ————————————————
11. ————————————————
12. ————————————————
13. ————————————————
14. ————————————————
15. ————————————————
16. ————————————————
17. ————————————————
18. ————————————————
19. ————————————————
20. ————————————————
21. ————————————————
22. ————————————————
23. ————————————————
24. ————————————————
25. ————————————————
26. ————————————————
27. ————————————————
28. ————————————————
29. ————————————————
30. ————————————————
31. ————————————————

Am I wrong?

Welsh National Anthem

Mae hen wlad fy Nhadau, yn annwyl i mi,
Gwlad beirdd a chantorion enwogion o fri;
Ei gwrol ryfelwyr, gwladgarwyr tra mad,
Dros ryddid collasant eu gwaed.
Gwlad, Gwlad, pleidiol wyf i'm gwlad;
Tra mor yn fur i'r bur hoff bau
O bydded i'r hen iaith barhau.

The old land of my fathers is dear to me,
Land of poets and singers, famous men of renown;
Its brave warriors, fine patriots,
Gave their blood for freedom.
My country, My country, I am devoted to my country,
While the sea is a wall to the pure loved land
O may the old language endure.

Written by EVAN JAMES of Pontypridd, his son composed the music.
First published in 1860. English words by DYFED WYN EDWARDS.

Calon Lân

Nid wy'n gofyn bywyd moethus
Aur y byd na'i berlau mân;
Gofyn 'rwyf am galon hapus,
Calon onest, calon lân.

[Cytgan]
Calon lân yn llawn daioni,
Tecach yw na'r lili dlos,
'Does ond calon lân all ganu,
Canu'r dydd a chanu'r nos.

Hwyr a bore fy nymuniad,
Esgyn ar adenydd cân.
Ar i Dduw er mwyn fy Ngeidwad,
Roddi imi galon lân.

[Cytgan]

I don't ask for luxurious life
The world gold or its fine pearls;
I ask for a happy heart,
An honest heart, a pure heart.

[Chorus]
A pure heart full of goodwill,
More lovely than the pretty lily,
Only a pure heart can sing,
Sing day and night.

Late and early my wish,
Rise to heaven on the wing of song.
To God, for the sake of my saviour,
Give me a pure heart.

[Chorus]

Conclusion

Looking out to Sea whilst fishing, you are watching our world breathing, one breath in and one breath out every 12 hours and 25 minutes. So it is up to us to look after our environment.

1. The Scientists are working on our global warming problem for the future, we **must** listen and take their advice.

2. Our Government is working on our limited fish stocks, they have a huge problem to overcome.

3. The SEA EMPRESS OIL TANKER became grounded on rocks off MILFORD HAVEN on the 15th February, 1996, spilling into the beautiful clean sea 72,000 tons *(yes 72,000 tons!)* of Crude oil, and 360 tons of heavy fuel oil into our marine environment. Chemical dispersants were sprayed, and a wide area of our Coastline became affected.

Lessons Must be learned that this under **no** circumstances be allowed to happen again.

4. OUR PROBLEM, right here, right now.

What really upsets me, is to see a Seagull with only one leg, or a length of fishing line sometimes with a hook still attached struggling along whilst in flight.

Every angler from time to time has a huge tangle of line 'BIRDNEST', but please do not just cut the line off and discard for the birds or other animals to get entangled. It takes no time to collect up your and other rubbish to take home and dispose of in the correct manor.

For eight or nine months of the year, sea anglers in the main have

the monopoly of our beaches, so can we please leave our beaches and rock venues in pristine condition, for our Summer visitors to learn from our example. So please again just leave your footprints.

Let it not be said that it is our generation that has destroyed our sport for our children and our childrens, children.

The P. C. Brigade are watching in the wings.

Every effort has been made to ensure accuracy in the writing of this small fishing book, but understandably things have changed since I started writing the book to it's publication. (e.g. Building a 'Jack Nicholas' designed golf course at MACHYNYS with rather expensive houses overlooking the golf course and beach, restricting the access. So please forgive me if I have made a few mistakes.

But one thing is for sure, your own safety is paramount.

Where the Tides of Fortune take us no one knows.

GOOD LUCK – GOD BLESS & BEST WISHES

Mal.

Author with sons Michael and Stephen.

Form 1

DATE

TIME

PLACE

WIND

N
E
W
S

○ CLEAR
○ CLOUDY
○ SEA MIST

CLIMATE

WATER
°C 0 10 20 30 40 50
32 50 70 90 110 °F

AIR
°C 0 10 20 30 40 50
32 50 70 90 110 °F

FORECAST

○
○
○

CATCH

BAIT

LINE

LENGTH

WEIGHT

NOTES

Form 2

DATE

TIME

PLACE

WIND

N
E
W
S

○ CLEAR
○ CLOUDY
○ SEA MIST

CLIMATE

WATER
°C 0 10 20 30 40 50
32 50 70 90 110 °F

AIR
°C 0 10 20 30 40 50
32 50 70 90 110 °F

FORECAST

○
○
○

CATCH

BAIT

LINE

LENGTH

WEIGHT

NOTES